Contents

Foreword...7

Dedication...9

Declaration by the Author 11

Taceat Mulier...!.....................................13

Chapter 1: The Story of This Book. Undertaken in 1879..21

Chapter 2: The Sublime Torrent......................27

Chapter 3: In Paradise................................31

Chapter 4: Louis-Philippe, September 19, 1846...37

Chapter 5: The Author's Design. Miracle of Universal Indifference...................................41

Chapter 6: God's Insuccess. The Apparent Failure of Redemption. The Most Sorrowful Sigh Since the Consummatum......................45

Chapter 7: Universal Refusal of Penance. "... Look, Mélanie, What They Have Done to Our Desert!... Ridebo et Subsannabo".................49

Chapter 8: The Sacred Heart Crowned with Thorns. Mary is the Queen of the Father......55

Chapter 9: You Knew, O My Lady of Transfixion, That I Do not Know How to Go About It...61

Chapter 10: Napoleon III Declares War on Mélanie..65

Chapter 11: Errant Life of the Shepherdess. Cardinal Perraud, Successor to Talleyrand, Divests Her..69

Chapter 12: The Priests and Mélanie's Secret 75

Chapter 13: Mary's Immense Dignity............79

Chapter 14: Identity of the Public Discourse and Mélanie's Secret. Eve's Lament............83

Persecution by Mgr. Fava. Disobedience, Criminal Infidelity of the Missionaries..........89

Chapter 16: Mélanie's Prophetic Gifts..........95

Chapter 17: Maximin's Prophetic Gifts.........99

Chapter 18: The Bishops of Grenoble at Soissons..107

Chapter 19: Profitable Sacerdocy. Vanity of Works in Full Disobedience. Punishments. Darkness..113

Chapter 20: The Woman Bent Over for 18 Years, Image of La Salette. Mary Speaks. Jesus no Longer Speaks then? The Immaculate Conception Crowned by Thorns, Stigmatized. Lourdes and La Salette..........119

Chapter 21: Profanation of Sunday.............127

Chapter 22: The Caterini Affair....................131

She Who Weeps
(Our Lady of La Salette)

… Little children under the age of seven will take to trembling and die in the arms of the people who hold them; others will do penance through hunger.

… The seasons will have changed...

– Words of the Holy Virgin.

LÉON BLOY

Translated By Richard Robinson

Sunny Lou Publishing Company
Portland, Oregon, USA
http://www.sunnyloupublishing.com

Corrected: January 1, 2024
1st Edition Corrected: December 2, 2021
Original Publication Date: October 11, 2021

ISBN: 978-1-955392-12-9

* * *

This translation from French is based on
the Société de Mercure de France edition of
Celle qui pleure, Paris, 1908.

Chapter 23: Mélanie's Sanctity. Apostles of the Last Days Prophesied by Her and by the Venerable Grignion de Montfort..................137

Chapter 24 Objections, Calumnies, the Assumptionist Drochon...............................145

Chapter 25: The Hostelry. The Missionaries or Chaplains' Double Tactic.........................151

Chapter 26: La Salette and Louis XVII........157

Appendices..163

Appendix 1: Documentary Evidence..........165

Appendix 2: Apparition of the Very Holy Virgin on the Mountain of La Salette..........209

Appendix 3: Funeral Oration........................253

Foreword

Sed ut perspiciatis, unde omnis iste natus error sit voluptatem accusantium doloremque laudantium, totam rem aperiam eaque ipsa, quae ab illo inventore veritatis et quasi architecto beatae vitae dicta sunt, explicabo. Nemo enim ipsam voluptatem, quia voluptas sit, aspernatur aut odit aut fugit, sed quia consequuntur magni dolores eos, qui ratione voluptatem sequi nesciunt, neque porro quisquam est, qui dolorem ipsum, quia dolor sit, amet, consectetur, adipisci velit, sed quia non numquam eius modi tempora incidunt, ut labore et dolore magnam aliquam quaerat voluptatem. Ut enim ad minima veniam, quis nostrum exercitationemullam corporis suscipit laboriosam, nisi ut aliquid ex ea commodi consequatur? Quis autem vel eum iure reprehenderit, qui in ea voluptate velit esse, quam nihil molestiae consequatur, vel illum, qui dolorem eum fugiat, quo voluptas nulla pariatur? [33] At vero eos et accusamus et iusto odio dignissimos ducimus, qui blanditiis praesentium voluptatum deleniti atque corrupti, quos dolores et quas molestias excepturi sint, obcaecati cupiditate non provident, similique sunt in culpa, qui officia deserunt mollitia animi, id est laborum et dolorum fuga. Et harum quidem rerum facilis est et expedita distinctio. Nam libero tempore, cum soluta nobis est eligendi optio, cumque nihil impedit, quo minus id, quod maxime placeat, facere possimus, omnis voluptas assumenda est, omnis dolor repellendus. Temporibus autem quibusdam et aut officiis debitis aut rerum necessitatibus saepe eveniet, ut et voluptates repudiandae sint et molestiae non recusandae. Itaque earum rerum hic tenetur a sapiente delectus, ut aut reiciendis voluptatibus maiores alias consequatur aut perferendis doloribus asperiores repellat.

– Cicero, 45 BC (*de Finibus Bonorum et Malorum*)

Dedication

To Pierre TERMIER,

Chief Engineer of the Mine Corps, Professor at the School of Mines.

This book has to be dedicated to you, my dear friend, for it would not exist without you. I had abandoned the project, twenty-seven years ago, and I had ended up no longer thinking about it, believing it impracticable.

Our Lady of Compassion was ever weeping on Her Mountain and I no longer heard her... She commanded that I be woken up by you.

We met in such a miraculous way! For thirty years you were waiting for someone who could speak to you about La Salette. I was waiting for the occasion to speak about her properly.

It happened finally that one day – not too long ago – having read some pages in one of my books, in which I was trying hard to glorify Our Lady of La Salette, it seemed to you that I could very well be the writer you had hoped for. We met not long thereafter and your impression, far from changing, became more precise.

Encouraged by you, seeing in you an ambassador of Mary, what better choice did I have than to obey? It was all I needed to face the difficulties and bitterness inherent in such a topic.

La Salette is still, after sixty years, the Fountain of Contradiction that is mentioned in the Holy Bible, and those who love her are called on to suffer.

Pass it on to all my My People, the Mother of God had said to the Shepherds, having announced to them the **Great News**.

At this time, I say to you: Pass my book on to the poor. You understand me well. I am speaking of that dolorous flock whom nobody thinks about and whom nobody shows any pity for: the generous people who do not know the Truth, the beautiful souls of vagabondage who would have need of a daily asylum...

"*Misereor super turbam*," said Jesus. Have pity on that flock who die of thirst at the banks of the rivers of Paradise.

Nativity of Mary, September 8, 1907.

– *LÉON BLOY*

Declaration by the Author

In my capacity as a Catholic, I declare to submit entirely to the doctrine of the Church, to the rules and decisions of the Holy See, notably to the decrees of Sovereign Pontiffs Urban VIII and Benedict XIV, concerning the canonization of the Saints.

If I should happen, while speaking of the two Shepherds of La Salette, to employ the words "saint," "saintly," or "sanctity," it is only in a purely relative sense, by insufficiency of language, for lack of terms that render my thought more completely. In advance, I disavow the rigorous and absolute meaning that one might wish to attribute to those expressions; for no one may be called a Saint as long as the Church has not qualified him or her as such, officially.

— *LÉON BLOY*

Taceat Mulier...![1]

I have just suffered through a terrible sermon against Materialism or Naturalism opposed to supernatural Revelation. All the philosophical commonplaces of the seminary were trotted out in front of the immobile Holy Sacrament. I had, alas! come to church like a "beggar filled with prayers." That gulf of vain expressions swallowed them up, and my soul slipped into the poor sleep that prattle procures. In the presence of the Enemy, this is what preachers come up with then, today, those who are raised for so long and cultivated with such care in contempt of the warnings of La Salette – on the eve of horrifying settlement dates!

How not to suppose a systematic deformation or a lack of faith in such ministers, and in such large numbers, when it gets to the point of their no longer knowing that at the core of man is Faith and Obedience and that, by consequence, what he needs are Apostles and not lecturers, Witnesses and not demonstrators. The time to prove that God exists is past. The hour sounds to give one's life to Jesus Christ.

Now, everyone energetically refuses to give it to him. To anyone else, but not Him! A demon rather! It is true that Christians have stopped believing in demons. Try – with the authority of the Gospel – to make it understood, for example, that wealth is a malediction, that it is impossible to serve both God and the world, that the so-called *charity bazaars* or gatherings invoke hell fire and that the beautiful

---

[1] *Taceat Mulier.* Latin for "Women should be quiet."

ladies or devotees who go there to find a last, truly infernal form of torture are servants of the devil, extremely attentive and duly recompensed! There will not be too great a change effected by what is usually and inexactly referred to as death, to discover suddenly, while letting out a cry loud enough to rip a hole through Eternity, at what point the most faithful among us were people lacking in faith.

"When France, muddied from head to toe," said Mélanie, "has been purified by the flogs of divine Justice, God will give her a *man*, but a *free man,* to rule over her. She will then be made to comply, nearly destroyed."

One would need to be gifted with a rare stupidity to go looking for that man among the livestock found at pilgrimages or Catholic congresses. Ah! I remember those crowds, the day after the war, in '73 exactly.

Their backsides were still smarting from the German boot. One spoke only of a return to God. One piled into Catholic circles to hear the good word of Mgr. Mermillod, recounting what he had suffered for Jesus Christ, or the œcumenical splutterings of M. de Mun. One latched on madly to the Count de Chambord, supposedly the great Monarch announced by the prophesies and whose *illegitimate* paunch was supposedly going to save everything. One rushed to pilgrimages, chanting liberating couplets. One voted for the erection of a sanctuary dedicated to the Sacred Heart on the walls of which these succorous words were written: *Gallia pœnitens et devota*,[2] and each person brought his own prayer, for that was the national Vow, strangely forgotten since then. What else? The Assumptionist[3] Fathers founded the prosperous *Pilgrim* and the profitable *Croix*,[4] for the irremediable debasement of Christian thought and sentiments. A little later, finally, was built, on the solid dungheap of hearts, a famous bank designed to absorb universal credit and to confound forever the competitive perfidy of the children of Israel.[5] That levy in mass of Catholic nest eggs was prodigiously called a *Crusade* and had, for its denouement, an immense *Crash* that is famous to this day.

Obedience to the Mother of God, who had come expressly, sixty years ago today, to notify us of her will, was the only expedient, which nobody paid any attention to.

But one could believe that all this was quite simple. The Sovereign of the universe was *upset*, if I dare say so, in the same way as the Milky Way would be upset if that incalculable creature, frightened by the nastiness of men, was found kneeling in the somber blue of the firmament. She went out of her

---

[2]*Gallia... devota*: Devoted and penitent Gaul.

[3]Assumptionists: Catholic fathers and brothers belonging to the congregation of Augustinians of the Assumption.

[4]*Pilgrim... Croix*: the first is a weekly journal, the second a daily, both still in existence today.

[5]Competitive perfidy of the children of Israel: the Jews were from the early Middle Ages allowed, unlike Catholics (at least officially), to practice "usury."

way to bring to us, while weeping,[6] the "great news" of the enormity of our danger. Speaking as only the Trinity can speak, that Ambassadress declared the imminence of chastisements and cataclysms and laid out exactly what needed to be done by men in order not to perish, for the menaces proffered by Her were *conditional* menaces, from these first words: **IF my people do not want to submit, I will be FORCED to let my Son's Arm go**.[7]

I repeat, what is simpler than to humble oneself and obey? One has done exactly the opposite. Mary had asked for observance of the Seventh Day and respect for her Son's Name. She wanted the laws of the Church to be observed and that her children, during Lent, not go to the butcher's shop "**like dogs**." She had confided to each of the two shepherds, to Mélanie principally, a secret of life and death, expressing her formal will – ratified since then by Pius IX and Leo XIII – that it should be passed on to all her people, after a determined period of time. Finally, she had given, *in French*, the Rule of a new religious Order: "the Apostles of the Last Days"... **the true disciples of God living and reigning in heaven; the true imitators of Christ made man; my children, my true devotees; those who have given themselves to me so that I might lead them to my divine Son; those whom I carry, so to speak, in my arms, those**

---

[6]Original footnote: *while weeping!* The Angels do not weep, but the Queen of Angels weeps, and it is for this reason that She is their Queen.

[7]Original footnote: "The people do not want to submit and the City of the Almighty is *forced!*" Imagine the Angels and the Saints letting out that cry of alarm in heaven!

**who have lived in my spirit; the Apostles of the
Last Days, the faithful disciples of Jesus Christ
who have lived in contempt of the world and themselves, in the poverty of silence, in prayer and
mortification, in chastity and in union with God,
in suffering and unknown to the world. It is time
that they come out and shine a light on the world...
For behold the time of times, the end of ends.**

Sixty years have passed. People have become
more profane, more blasphemous, more disobedient,
more like "dogs."[8] But does it not seem to you that
that incomprehensible insuccess, that monstruous fi-
asco, but adorable for all that, of the Empress of Paradise, has had no noticeable effect on anything whatsoever, when one thinks of the irremissible Derision
that has replaced Obedience.

People work on Sundays more and more and
the poor, above all, are made to work. Blasphemy has
become a virile toga, even for women, a sign of
strength and independence, like tobacco or alcohol.
One had the ambition of being a *dog*, the son of a dog
and even a pig's nephew, at every time of the year,
indistinctly, and that ambition was the last straw.
Mary's words which She wanted to be passed on to
all Her people, as well in Tibet or the Terra del Fuego
as in Isère, did not go noticeably much farther than
the foot of the Mountain. As for the Apostles of the
Last Days, they were replaced by soup-merchant ecclesiastics whom the pilgrims could appreciate.

Those so-called missionaries were the inexpi-

---

[8]Original footnote: *Dog.* I recall that this was the expression that it
pleased the Mother of God to use.

able derision just mentioned. Absolute Disobedience is an incomprehensible state as long as the idea of *derision* does not present itself to the mind. The initial Fall must have been triggered not by formal disobedience, but by a *derisory obedience,* the which we can have no idea of, and, because abyss invokes abyss, the chastisement was – in appearance at least – an immense Derision, a biblical Subsannation: "Behold Adam, who was like us..."

The self-styled missionaries of La Salette, innocent perhaps, by dint of doltishness and baseness of heart, – but with what frightening innocence! – were, I repeat, a derisory institution put forward by diocesan authority in opposition to formal Commandment in an attempt at elusion. The Holy Virgin had asked for Apostles. She was given innkeepers.[9] She had wanted true disciples of Jesus Christ, with disdain for the world and for themselves. Instead, merchant-priests, pious accountants were installed, charged with *turning a profit.* As for the encouragement to "come out and shine a light on the world," they went about it by advertising [merchandise and services] and shaking the pilgrims down...

After sweeping away the mercenaries in 1902, the chaplains who replaced them simply continued the offering of room and board.[10] They continued also the quotidian and stereotypic recitation of the Miracle coupled with a *Sulpician* exhortation for the practice

---

[9]Original footnote: On the topic of male and female innkeepers, see chapter XXV of the present work.

[10]Original footnote: see chapter XXV.

of some reasonable virtues, while including the frequent advice to distrust certain exaggerated or deceitful publications, such as the written testimony of the two shepherds who were the witnesses, the auditors, the true missionaries selected by the Holy Virgin herself to propagate her warnings and her threats and who, until their dying day, have not stopped, Mélanie principally, to protest against the sacerdotal prevarications and hateful mercantilism practiced on the Mountain.

The crime of all those people, an enormous crime, quite terrible really, is to have gagged the Queen of Heaven, to have *sealed* her lips, as someone wrote recently with frightful energy.

It is difficult, I do not say to imagine, but to conceive of, so lamentable a supplication:

"For as long as I have suffered for you others; for nineteen centuries as I carry through the mountains the Seven Sorrows that I am the Shepherdess of, the seven sheep of the Holy Ghost who must, one day, graze the world; **if I do not want my Son to abandon you, I am weighed down with praying continuously**; what can I do for you that I have not done? I am Egypt and the Red Sea; I am the Desert and the Manna; I am the gorgeous Vine, but I am, at the same time, divine Thirst and the Lance that pierces the Savior's Heart. I am the infinitely dolorous Flagellation, I am the Crown of Thorns, and the Nails, and above all I am the very hard Cross where the joy of men is begotten. My Son's two Arms were attached to it, but only one is needed to crush you, and I cannot hold it back any longer, – it is so heavy!... Ah! my children, if only you converted!..."

The men of that time stood up, those who wore a miter on their head and held the shepherd's staff of Christ's flock in their hands. And those men said to Our Lady:

"Enough of that talk, eh? *Taceat Mulier in Ecclesia!*[11] We are Bishops, Doctors of Divinity, and we have no need of anyone, not even the People in God. We are, besides, friends of Caesar and we do not want any disturbances among the people. Your menaces do not trouble us the least in the world and your little shepherds will get nothing from us, not even in their old age, save disdain, calumny, derision, persecution, misery, exile, and oblivion finally!..."

The hope of the present work is to repair, in some manner and *if there is still time*,[12] the perfidious sacrilege of those Caiaphases and those Judases who have destroyed, for sixty years now, the most beautiful kingdom in the world.

– Paris-Montmartre, February 1907.

---

[11] *Taceat Mulier in Ecclesia!* Latin for "Women should be quiet in church!"

[12] If there is still time: the emphasis is on the part of the editor.

Chapter 1: The Story of This Book. Undertaken in 1879

I made the pilgrimage to La Salette formerly, no more than thirty years ago, before the railroad from Grenoble to Mure existed. A homicidal diligence yoked to twelve horses, on certain ascents, broke the travelers' back, from sunrise to sunset, on the longest days. We moaned and groaned for ten hours before being handed over to the muleteers.

It was quite nice like that, moreover. Many tourists grew weary of it, but the landscape was affectionate and consoling for the pilgrim. At certain places, one got down to give the animals a rest, and it was an exquisite sweetness to walk along slowly under the tall trees, with the sound of the water currents that rushed through the ravines. I will always remember those several hundred steps, in the company of a missionary who had, I believe, a certain genius and who told me, in extraordinary words, the majesty of the Holy Texts. He passed away, three weeks later, having asked the Mother of God for a long time to end his days up there at La Salette, where he was buried. He had had enough of the hideousness of this world and the contemporary pharisaical piety that seemed to him like an apostasy.

I will not name that priest. His family is too

unworthy of him, but I know what he gave me, *dum loqueretur in via et aperiret mihi Scripturas*.[13] I saw his grave again, the following year, a humble cross on a humble mound of grass; then again, last year, twenty-six years later, but abandoned, his remains having been transferred to a vault recently constructed two paces away from there, where his name, well-known among the Angels and some friends of God, can be read.

That missionary, more orator than writer, had traveled the world, announcing the Glory of the Mother of Jesus Christ, and it was always to La Salette that he returned, to draw, at the feet of She Who Weeps, inspiration for his apostolic zeal.

The Discourse, infinitely extraordinary, that the children heard on that Mountain, had become the center of his thoughts, and the intelligence that he had of it was like one of those inexpressible gifts that the Venerable Grignion de Montfort attributed prophetically to the Apostles of the Last Days.

One could make a name for oneself as an exegete on nothing but the crumbs of the feast offered daily to the listeners of that very humble man, when he spoke about the Queen of Patriarchs and Martyrs. The type of mysterious disfavor that weighs down on La Salette in the minds of a great number of Christians broke his heart. The present book, undertaken and begun under his guidance, at La Salette even, was interrupted for a quarter of a century, God knows how and why. That work of justice was his supreme de-

---

[13]*dum... Scripturas*: Latin for, "while he spoke along the way he revealed the Scriptures to me."

sire, his hope.

He died after the first pages were written, as if the Consolatrice whom he served did not want that really sacerdotal and crucified soul to lose, in some manner, the sorrowful aureole that she places around the face of those victims of Love that are spoken of in the Third Beatitude, and who cannot be consoled on earth.

That work, which I take up again today, appears even more difficult and fearsome than before. The death of the man who inspired me to the task overwhelmed me with a mourning that I thought irreparable, and the most miserable life that could be imagined turned me away finally, indefinitely.

The time was not right. What could I do then if not an exegetic and literary paraphrase of the Discourse at best? Too many things were unknown to me. I was ignorant even of the Secret of Mélanie, published only in November 1879, and so impenetrably obnubilated by the sacerdotal fear that to this day even nearly all Catholics are ignorant of it or biased against it.

Then, wasn't it necessary to wait for the French Republic's turpitudes and congenital ignominies to accumulate to such a point now that one wonders how death figures into it? Haven't all the demons already risen like a single demon to invoke the complete blossoming of the stinking democratic flower, so laboriously acclimated by those in the Kingdom which was the birthplace of Christian Authority? Finally and above all the *Heavy Arm* of Justice, must it not wait for the sixty-times-outraged Ambassadress in tears to say to her Son: "I no longer recognize this people, it has become too horrible"?

After so long a time, my name having become almost famous, some ardent people believed that I could really be designated to write on La Salette the book that certain souls need, – a pious book that would not be hostile to divine magnificence, a book that would say, after sixty years, several plausible words on that unprecedented Event, absolutely misunderstood and *ignored* even by the so-called missionaries, and the secular priests who succeeded them, on the Mountain.

"Pass it on to all my people," said, two times, the All-Ineffable One. And that is what gnawed away at my initiator. "Who thinks about it then?" he said to me, "and what could one pass on to all the people, that is to say to all men? The people of this place, – do they even know what has happened in this place? and the best among them – is he able to understand one word, one single word even of that Discourse that appears to be the *Verbum novissimum* of the Holy Ghost?"

Alas! the explanation, irremediably lost, that that man could have given, will be, from now on, what it can be: an anguishing vision of the present times with respect to the promises and equally scorned threats made by the Mother of the Son of God – vision of terror enormously aggravated by acquired certitude and completely incontestable of certain preliminary events. What does it matter, after all, if my thus mutilated work can still contain enough of that vanished word to attract to La Salette some of those magnificent souls capable of feeling the beauty, even through the obscurities or weaknesses of an insufficient predication?

I would have wanted to be able to tell them, like Bossuet speaking in front of the King of France's peruke: "Listen, believe, profit hereby, I will break the bread of life for you"; but so lofty a manner of speaking, – would it not, on the contrary, put off in the surest fashion a great number of hearts already subjugated, unbeknownst to themselves, by the luxurious Prince with the Crushed Head who does not stop promising his slaves the sovereign empire that he himself has been dispossessed of?... What a triumph to succeed merely at making contemporaries of the automobile catch a glimpse of the Splendor!

The Jerusalem priest, the missionary whom I just spoke of, was named Louis-Marie-René, and that is already much more than I had wished to reveal. Would that the patronage then of this book, which will be above all a book of sorrow, be like him. La Salette is, par excellence, the Place of very sorrowful tears.

One recalls that when the Apparition stopped speaking to the children, there was an extraordinary drama. The resplendent Lady, whose Feet, by the testimony of her puerile listeners, did not touch the ground but "touched only the tips of the grass," moves away from them slowly by a sort of gliding movement, and, after having crossed over the rivulet that came between her and the steep slope of the plateau, She begins to delineate that surprising *ser-*

pentine Itinerary, marked today by those Fourteen Crosses of the difficult Way which seems to superimpose itself in the translucid meditation of bleeding Mysteries...

That unique way of the cross had been decreed, like all things, anteriorly to the creation of spaces. It entered into the entirety of the divine Plan that the kneelings of the last Christian inhabitants on earth should be determined, with that precision, in that savage place, by the furrow left by those Feet of light. It is not an indifferent matter to prostrate oneself there or elsewhere. Religious souls who come to weep at La Salette do a thing that harmoniously resounds in the complete series of divine Decrees touching on the Redemption of humanity. Their tears fall on that privileged soil, like the sowing of many other tears that will finish, God willing, by flowing there, one day, like waves. "The abyss of Mary's Tears invokes the abyss of our tears by the Voice of her cataracts." She provokes us to that effusion just as her Son, high up on the Cross, provoked her passionately Himself – to the total effusion of her incomparable and broken Heart.

Chapter 2: The Sublime Torrent

I return to my voyage. So no more cruel diligence rolling along for an entire day. Only half the old fatigue and the other half like a dream. Oh! that railroad at the edge of a gulf, for one hour! What intoxication to go out like that to meet Napoleon Bonaparte marching from Sisteron on Grenoble, through Corps and La Mure! Corps above all, the archpriestese[14] of La Salette!

Chance having nothing to do with it, one can stuporously imagine "the eagle" of that conqueror "flying towards Paris from steeple to steeple," but descending from that of Corps in order to cry, thirty-one years before Our Lady: "My children, do not be afraid, I am here to announce to you some great news!" Then this: "You will pass it on to all my people." How not to pass it on?

The great man and his faithful companions appeared to be all France for twenty days, all that France was possible of, all human and divine eventuality of that angelic fatherland, of that eldest Daughter of the Son of God and his Church, of that inhabitant of his Heart's Wound, who could not fall any lower except by becoming the Magdalene of nations!

---

[14]archpriestese: a nonce word here for the territorial jurisdiction of an archpriest. In French, archiprêtré.

The poor escapee of Caesar, incorrigible beggar of universal domination, was surrounding without
knowing it, in the manner of Prototypes, the undis-
closed future of countrysides or villages that could
not have any historical existence unless such a passer-
by willed it. I have sought him here and there, and I
confess that his memory was greater than the eternal
mountains for me. Only, did he see them? Did he see
the Drac, that formidable torrent, the glory of the
Dauphiné? I doubt it. One torrent looks like any other, and the mountain itself was merely an obstacle for
him in which it roared within its depths.

A pilgrim of La Salette and nothing but that,
waiting for the honor to kneel before the Sacred
Tomb, I looked at it and saw it up close, that furious
torrent, with an admiration that suffocated me. How
many centuries were needed for that water to hollow
out so vast a bed in that grandiose solitude? For im-
measurable years, it must have gnawed away at the
rocks and dug out the gulfs, while foaming. As generations were born and died, while History unfolded,
under the Allobroges and the Romans, under the Bur-
gundians, the Franks, or the Saracens, under the lords
d'Albon and the first Valois, during the atrocious
wars of religion, during the Revolution, during the astonishing Empire and until our days when the Desired
One had to appear, – indefatigably, the ever young
water chipped away at the hard strata, riddled them
with the artillery of its pebbles, sapped the colossal
colonnades at their base, creating the continuous
abyss that splits in two that lofty Dauphinois province, ancient apanage of the eldest sons of France: the

Grésivaudan,[15] Royannès, Baronnies,[16] Gapençois, Embrunois, Briançonnais, from the Durance to the Isère,[17] that monstruous flock of green croups or bare peaks whose names God only knows!

The train for La Mure, coming from Grenoble, rolls I don't know how many kilometers along the length of that enormous fent procured by the Drac above which one has the illusion of being suspended. Clamor from below that is never interrupted in the time of rains or melting snow.

A morose and sterilized novelist[18], several years ago, wanted to avenge himself of the base fear that that cry from the abyss had fill him with. Stupidly and villainously he went out of his way to disparage it by his adjectives and his miserable metaphors, comparing that sublime water to "a debile, maleficent, rotten... river." That poor man, who must have pleased many of La Salette's enemies, blames the mountains naturally and shows himself to be extremely far from approving the circumstances or the details of the Apparition, which would have taken place in plain sight, in the vicinity of a train station and much more simply, if one had had one's druthers. *In die ju-*

---

[15]Grésivaudan: a valley in the Dauphiny, and from which comes the name Grenoble, the capital city.

[16]Baronnies, Gapençois, Embrunois, Briançonnais: all natural, historical regions in the Dauphiny.

[17]Durance... Isère: the names of two rivers, the Isère named after the Isérois people who lived there thousands of years B.C.

[18]novelist: J.-K. Huysmans in his *The Cathedral*.

dicii, libera nos, Domine.[19]

I hope that my panting admiration for that magnificent spectacle will be counted in my favor. Why would one wish that God were not an artist like anyone else, jealous of his work and desirous that people admire it? Does he not speak, at every instant, of his "holy mountains" that he has "prepared in his strength" and whose "heights are his own"? *Ego sum Dominus faciens omnia et nullus mecum.*[20] There was no question of others' mountains, only his own, and he insists that one adore him for having made them.

Does a more marvelously scenic path exist for pilgrims' admiration as they mend their way up to a shrine? I do not think so. Formerly, it was not like this. The route that diligences followed was not bestride a precipitous ravine. That unique railway was needed, that masterwork of men, in order to reveal to us the masterwork of nature that God had made known previously only to some locals. I saw it again, on my return visit, lit up, that time, in full moonlight, the moon riddling the immense landscape with its silver rays, and I thought I was in Paradise.

---

[19] *In dii... Domine*: Latin for, "In days of judgment, free us, Lord." From the "Kyrie eleison," an important processional Litany, or Rogation, forming part of the liturgy of the Roman Catholic Church and dating back to the earliest days of the church. Also known as the Litany of the Saints.

[20] *Ego... mecum*: Latin for, "I am the Lord that maketh all things; ... by myself," (KJV), Isaiah 44:24.

Chapter 3: In Paradise

In Paradise! Before going any further, would it be inappropriate to explore in some manner, as much as possible, that "region of peace and light," that "seat – that capital – of refreshment and beatific consolation," that earthly paradise in the skies?

Here, the indigence of my human speech is enough to make one cry. Everything that is not body, space, or duration is inexpressible to the point that the Verb of God himself, Our Lord Jesus Christ, has never spoken but in parables and similitudes.[21] It is man's destiny to be unable to wrest his heart from the famous Place of Voluptuousness whence he was ignominiously expelled at the beginning of time. He needs Paradise to be a *place*, a very lofty or very lowly place, and we are forced, in the first case, to say that the Holy Virgin came down from there to weep at La Salette. Mélanie has described the childish paradise that she constructed, September 19, with Maximin, one moment before the Apparition: a large rock they had covered in flowers. It is on that paradise that the Beautiful Lady came to sit. The Queen of Enoch's and the Good Thief's Paradise, which is the incomprehensible Bosom of Abraham where, in order to understand the unrevealable Arcana, the immense Doctor of nations was ravished; – that Queen is attracted by the extreme puerility of that paradise that the little shepherds had made. "She had looked the world over," said Mélanie, "and found nothing baser. She

---

[21]Original footnote: Testimony of the Evangelist Saint Mark, 13:34.

had no other choice but me."

Paradise is so such and in so many ways at the threshold of the Miracle of La Salette, that is also impossible to speak about it without saying one worthwhile thing about it. That paradise is clearly the Beautiful Lady herself, but that is too facile. One may as well proclaim the identity of God by one or more of his attributes. The foundation of Paradise, or of the idea of Paradise, is a union with God in the present life, in other words an infinite Distress in the heart of man, and a union with God in the future Life, which is Beatitude. The mode of it is infinitely unknown and undivinable, but one can, to a certain point, be contented in one's mind by the extremely plausible hypothesis of an *eternal ascension*, an endless ascension of Faith, Hope, Love.

Ineffable contradiction! One will believe more and more, knowing that one shall never understand; one will hope more and more, assured never to attain; one will love more and more what can never be possessed.

It is well understood that I am expressing myself like an impotent person. *Secundum hominem dico*.[22] Union with God is certainly realized by the Saints, in the present life, and perfectly consummated soon after their birth in the other Life, but that does not suffice for them and that does not suffice for God. The most intimate union with God is not enough, there must be *identification* which will never itself be enough, in the sense that Beatitude cannot be con-

---

[22]*Secundum hominem dico*: Latin for "I speak as a man."

ceived or imagined except as an always more vivid, more impetuous, more stunning ascension, not towards god, but in God, in the Essence even of the Uncircumscribed. Theological hurricane without end or repose that the Church, speaking to men, is forced to call *Requies æterna!*[23]

The unchained crowd of Saints is comparable to an immense army of tempests, rushing at God with a vehemence capable of uprooting the nebulae, and that for all eternity... Can astronomical reveries be utilized here? The inconceivable enormity of figures charged with signifying the frightening hyperboles of Distance or Speed would help all the more to get a glimpse of the impossibility of understanding "what God has prepared for those who love him." One could say even, given it is a matter of Infinity and Eternity, that he must have a continual accelerator for each torrent analogous to the head-spinning multiplication of the *gravity* of falling bodies. A paralyzed Mysticism, that a highly abstract imagery encourages, localizes the Saints in the hieratic attitude promulgated by Institutes, under the immovable aureole that no breeze shall ever displace, and among the gold or silver utensils of piety that neither rust nor worms will gnaw at. For such is the idea that can be formed of Paradise and the Felicity of the Saints, of Catholics engendered by the acephalous escapees of last century's guillotine.

But how vain, lamentably infirm are the literary analogies or metaphysical conjectures of a poor writer bent on the Unsoundable and not obtaining

---

[23]*Requies æterna*: Latin for "eternal repose."

even the energy of intuition that he would need to discern, for one instant, at the risk of dying of fright, the vertiginous abyss of contemporary Unintelligence!

Requiem æternam dona eis, Domine,[24] that is: Give those souls, Lord, the wherewithal to engage in infinite battle whereby each of them, like a cataract in reverse, will eternally besiege you.

A dear pious soul asked this: "In that universal ascension, what would become of the mediocre, the poor men who, having done nothing for God in this world, will have been, nonetheless, saved by the effect of an ineffable encounter with Justice and Glory? What will become of those people who, having loved the beautiful things of the world, Poetry, Art, War, Voluptuousness even, find themselves all of a sudden face to face with the Absolute, not having prepared at all for their passage, but saved all the same, their hands empty?" They will need, under pain of eternal inanition, immediately, and *absolutely*, to realize everything that they are missing, and Wisdom will provide for them. Beauty, having become a vulture, will carry them away, endlessly, in order to devour them forever and always, those who will have really loved it under any appearance whatsoever.

Assuredly, it will be just like that, and more than one poet will be surprised for having been, unbeknownst to himself, so great a friend of God! But must he be mixed together with the mediocre types because of unobserved Commandments,? That punition would be enormous, and the thought of it is mon-

---

[24]*Requiem... Domine*: Latin for "Give them all eternal life, Lord."

struous. The truth, infinitely probable, is that one or another of them will take the stage particularly suited to himself, with admirable discernment.

And then there will be a firmament of unimaginable, differentiated splendors. The Saints will rise towards God like lightning, supposing it multiplied on its own initiative, at every second, throughout the centuries, their charity constantly growing at the same time as their brightness, indescribable Stars that those who have known only the Face of Jesus Christ but who have been ignorant of his Heart will follow from an enormous distance. As for the stars, the poor, so-called *practicing* Christians, observers to the facile Letter, but not perverse, and capable of a certain generosity, they will follow in their turn, not getting lost, the billions of cavalcades of lightning, having previously paid an inexpressible price for their seats, joyous all the same – infinitely more than the rarest lexicons of happiness could express – and joyous precisely for the incomparable glory of their elder brothers and sisters, joyous in depth and in breadth, joyous like the Lord when he succeeded in creating the world!

And everyone, as I have said, will climb together like a tempest without lull, the fortunate tempest of the interminable end of ends, an assumption of cataracts of love, and such will be the Garden of Voluptuousness, the indescribable Paradise spoken of in the Scriptures.

Earlier I mentioned Mélanie and Maximin's paradise. Just now I have mentioned mine, such as it is. Would that it might, as theirs did, make the Holy

Virgin come down and visit me!

Chapter 4: Louis-Philippe, September 19, 1846

"It is about two-thirty in the afternoon. The King, the Queen, their Royal Highnesses, Mme. the Princess Adélaïde, Mgr. the Duke and Mme. the Duchess of Nemours, the Prince Philippe of Wurtemberg and the Count of Eu, accompanied by M. the Minister of Public Instruction, the Generals de Chabannes, de Lagrange, de Ressigny, M. the Colonel Dumas and many officers of ordonnance, go outside to promenade in the park. After their promenade, Their Majesties and Their Highnesses return to the chateau at about five o'clock in the evening to dine, while waiting for the evening *illuminations*."

It is in this way that a correspondent full of diligence, in a dispatch addressed from Ferté-Vidame, announces to the *Universal Monitor* the most considerable event of the day on September 19, 1846.[25]

I am, happily, in a position to remind the universe of that event which it appears to have forgotten. At a distance of more than sixty years, it is not without interest to contemplate, by imagination or memory, that July promenade of the king accompanied by his crew in a decent park, in view of working up an appetite before dinner and preparing himself, by a naïve spectacle of nature, for the municipal magnificences of the evening's illumination.

---

[25]Original footnote: *Monitor,* September 21, 1846.

That historic divertissement put into the perspective of the other Royal Promenade that was happening at the same time on the mountain of La Salette, is, I think, of a nature to strongly arrest one's thought. The really Biblical contrast of such a comparison is not expected to augment the already mediocre prestige of that gloriless monarchy, born in the liberal quagmire of 1830 and predestined to die out dishonorably in the economical sewer of 1848. I would be curious to know what was going on in the Royal Citizen's soul at the very moment that the Queen of Heaven, all in tears, manifested herself before two children in an unknown corner of that beautiful France polluted and dying under the abject domination of that thaumaturge of debasement.

He was strolling under the plane trees and chestnut trees, dreaming or speaking of a sixteen-year reign's great things and of the magnificent results of an administration exempt from that honorable fanaticism that had paralyzed, formerly, the generous rise of revolutionary liberalism. Everything was working out as desired, externally as well as internally. By an amendment that remains famous in parliamentary splendors, the count de Morny claimed that the great Bodies of State were satisfied. God and the Pope were suitably outraged, despicable Jesuitism was finally at its last breath, and the nation governed by laws had no other wish than to see eternalized, in a rather beneficial dynasty, the unhoped-for felicities of that adorable government. One was finally going to marry Spain, one was going to become huge. In the example of Charles V and Napoleon, the patriarch of Orleanism could aspire to universal domination. The belly of the bitch had, moreover, grown sufficiently large and Their Highnesses caracoled rather nobly around His Majesty in the autumnal breeze of that serene September day. The king of the French could say, like the prophet of the land of Hus: "I will die in the bed I made for myself, and I will multiply my days like the palm tree; I am like a tree whose roots extend along the waters, and the dew will descend on my branches. My glory will be renewed day after day, and my bow will grow stronger in my hand."[26]

At two hundred leagues away, the Mother of God weeps bitterly over her people. If Their Majesties and Their Highnesses could, for one instant, deign to assume the attitude that was fitting for them, that is to say to lie prostrate in the dirt and put their ears, inattentive until then, close to the ground, perhaps that humble and faithful creature would transmit to them some strange, distant sound of the threats and sobs that would make them turn pale. Perhaps also their dinner would have been without drunkenness and their illumination without hope...

While Orleanism was patting itself on the back in the evening, the two shepherds chosen to represent all majesties, living or dead, triumphant or fallen, approached *their* Queen. It was at that moment that the dolorous Mother raised her voice above the indistinct murmur of the hymn of Swords[27] which was being sung around Her in ten thousand churches:

---

[26]Original footnote: Job 24:18-20.

[27]Original footnote: Hymn *O quot undis lacrymarum*, feast of Our Lady of Seven Sorrows.

If My people do not want to submit, I will be forced to let My Son's Arm go...

Chapter 5: The Author's Design. Miracle of Universal Indifference.

The design of this work, clearly indicated in the introduction, is not to tell the story of the Miracle of La Salette. That has been told so often that Christians are to be excused for ignoring it. Having grown up, the two shepherds themselves have written about it and published it, and their two narrations, which ought to have been disseminated everywhere, are identical in the circumstances of the Event and the text of public Discourse. As for the *Secrets*, Mélanie alone has divulged hers, leaving for the Sovereign Pontiff the Rule, *given by Mary*, of a new religious Order, the Order of the "Apostles of the Last Days," a foundation clearly prophesied in the 17th century, by the Venerable Grignion de Montfort.

Not writing for the multitude, I address myself then exclusively to those who know the Facts of La Salette, assured that others were not interested. I want above all to show, as well as I can, the miracle that followed and which is perhaps greater than that of the Apparition, – the miracle, certainly more incredible, of a large number of people's universal indifference or hostility.

Those children's voices that, descending from the

Alps, were supposed to grow in size like an avalanche and cover the Earth, – one has tried to stifle them as much as one could. "Pass it on to my people," the Sovereign had said. The Jews themselves would be surprised by so complete a disobedience. The first Pastors have not mounted their cathedra to announce the Great News to their diocesans, the Preachers and Missionaries of every Institute have not been mobilized enthusiastically to make known the threats and promises of the Omnipotent One to those most ignorant. Many have done just the opposite with an infernal malice. The words fallen from that quasi divine Mouth that pronounced the FIAT of the Incarnation, those so terrible and so maternal Words, they were not taught at school, and children the same age as the shepherds have not learnt them. One knows, a little bit everywhere, vaguely, that La Salette exists, that the Holy Virgin manifested herself there in a certain manner, and that She said something. Divers persons know even that the profanation of Sunday and Blasphemy have been singularly condemned by Her. But the *text* of that Discourse, one does not find it in anyone's memory, nor in hand. As for the Secrets, one does not even want to hear them spoken.

Eh, well! It's enough to frighten the daylights out of someone. Jesus Christ suffers when one contemns him or when one outrages him. We are exactly at the twentieth century of slaps and spits that fall without amnesty, for two thousand years now, on the immensely holy Face, constituting thus what one calls the Christian Era. But he will not suffer his Mother to be disdained, his Mother in tears!... She about whom the Church sings that she was "conceived before the mountains and the gulfs and before the eruption of springs";[28] that "mystical City full of people, sitting in solitude and weeping without anyone consoling it";[29] that moaning "Dove hidden in the clefts of the rock";[30] that Queen of Heaven, weeping like an abundance in the fold of the rock and almost unable anymore to hold herself up, because of sorrow, after having been so strong on the other Mountain!...

Alone, on that mysteriously prepared rock that reminds one of the other Rock on which the Church is built; her Breast filled with images of Her Child's instruments of torture and weeping as one has not wept for two thousand years: **Since I have been suffering for you others who do not care**, She said.

Imagine for yourself that sorrowful Mother seated on that rock, continuing to sob in that ravine and *never* once rising, until the end of the world! One will have some idea then of what subsists eternally under the Eye of Him whose Mother she is and for whom not one thing is past or future. Try finally to gauge the power of that perpetual clamor from such a Mother to such a Son and, at the same time, the absolutely inexpressible indignation of such a Son against the authors of such a Mother's tears! All that one can say or write on the subject does not come even close...

---

[28]Original footnote: Proverbs 8:24-25.

[29]Original footnote: Thren. I:1-2.

[30]Original footnote: Song of Songs 2:14.

Chapter 6: God's Insuccess. The Apparent Failure of Redemption. The Most Sorrowful Sigh Since the *Consummatum*

Now see where we find ourselves! Mary's Tears and her Words have been so perfectly hidden, for sixty years, that Christianity ignores them finally. Her Son's frightening Anger was not suspected, even by those who eat his Flesh and drink his Blood, and the world keeps on keeping on. However, numerous prophesies, particularly unanimous, affirm that our epoch is singled out for God's appeasement, which will be the Deluge of Catastrophes. That, after having caught a glimpse of it or guessed at it only, is enough to turn heads and even globes.

The enormity of the case would necessitate an archangelic power of vision. After nineteen centuries of Christianity, as much to say one hundred generations, soaked in the Blood of Christ! And for what? The twentieth century can ask itself that question stuporously. The fierce optimism that presumes the Gospel announced to all nations from now on is only sustainable in *good news* articles or in the lowest-tier elementary classes, before teaching the basics of the simplest geography. The too certain truth is that, out of the fourteen or fifteen hundred million human beings who populate our globe, at most one third know of the Name of Jesus Christ, and ninety-nine percent of that third know it in vain. As to the quality of those remaining, it is an infinitely mysterious shame, a prodigy of sorrow assimilable only by the incomprehensible Septenary of Sorrows of Mary's Compassion.

The *apparent* reality is the insuccess of God on earth, the failure of the Redemption. The visible results are so appalling in insignificance, and become all the more insignificant with each passing day, that one has to wonder, crazy as it may sound, whether the Savior has not abdicated. "*Quæ utilitas in sanguine meo, dum descendo in corruptionem?*"[31] There we have it, for what it is worth, the Agony in the Garden, such as the ecstatics had seen it! Ah! it really was worth it to bleed so much and to groan so much, to receive so many slaps, so many spits, so many blows of the whip, to be so frightfully crucified! It really was worth it to be the Son of God and to die the son of man in order to end up, after having been trampled under by all the demons for nineteen centuries, at present-day Catholicism!

I know that there have been Saints, one perhaps for every ten million inhabitants on the globe, especially formerly, and it appears rather clear that that suffices for God, provisionally at least, but how

---

[31]*Quæ... corruptionem*: Latin for, "What good is my blood, while I sink in corruption?"

could that suffice for us and how content us, we others who do not see the causes? One tells us – with such rigor! – that anything not of the Church are lost. Now, many more than one hundred thousand men are born each day who will *never* hear tell of the Church nor of a God whatsoever, even in the so-called Christian world, and that one rots from the cradle... I have lived long and sorrowful months among Luther's people, in one of the three Scandinavian kingdoms, and I have seen the impossibility of knowing the Truth – one hundred times more insurmountable than among the pagans. And God knows however whether his terrible Name is spoken there!

What to say, after that, of the innumerable idolatries among which it would be unjust not to count traditional Catholics entrenched in the inexpugnable certitude that they are sifted through, picked out grain by grain, like the wheat for the Eucharist, and that penance is not for them? They above all are frightening. The pure savages of Africa or Polynesia, the human fruits of hideous asiatic cultures, the monstruous polymorphs of the most debased intellectuality, of the most dethroned reason; all those unfortunate peoples have their gods of wood or stone, some of which are so demoniacal and so dark that one can neither laugh nor weep when one sees them. However, let Jesus Christ be shown on his Cross and the majority of them, instantly, will become gulfs of humility.

The idol of honorable Catholics which I have just spoken about is precisely the same Cross, but placed by them on the shoulders, and on the heart, of the Poor. They would renounce it if they had to carry it themselves. In its place, they adore it, and "the Sweat of Jesus falls to the ground in drops of blood"...

Non fecit taliter omni nationi. You said it yourself, Lord. We are the privileged nation, the chosen flock. It is for us that you died, and we have merely to let ourselves live. The martyrs and penitents were needed, in the past, in order to install ourselves in this spiritual and material comfort which is probably the mirror of the Angels. What better things have we got to do than to be generous and sweet amongst ourselves and to enjoy your gifts, while despising as is fitting the prophesies or the threats disapproved of by our pastors?

Evidently Our Lady of La Salette says nothing and has nothing to say to such Christians.

Will the Mother of God need to walk in vain then on the mountains? The Discourse of La Salette is the saddest sigh heard since the *Consummatum*. Who would dare say that the Virgin is "happy" to see the Blood of her Son spilt in vain, after so many centuries, and where is the Seraph that would delimit that torment?

Chapter 7: Universal Refusal of Penance. "... Look, Mélanie, What They Have Done to Our Desert!... *Ridebo et Subsannabo*"

"The place where you tread is a holy land," it was said to Moses on Horeb, "the mountain of God." I found that phrase on the walls of the inn at La Salette. Assuredly, it is in the right place, but the rest of the Text would be needed: "*Solve calceamentum de pedibus tuis*": Take off your shoes.

No one would come anymore. It is a real Penance. It is not only about one's feet, and what feet! It is about the indispensable need to bare one's soul and one's heart. And all the world flees! The so-called missionaries and, after them, the present chaplains have anticipated it. *Ne quid nimis!* Don't overdo it. Far from asking too much, one contrives to ask for nothing at all, and the result exceeds all expectations.

"Threats in the mouth of Mary, who's so good and so sweet!" a young mother said to me the other day; "threats against the weak, innocent and pure children! and threats of death, atrocious death!... No!

no!... Mary is a mother, she cannot say such things. She knows only how to love, vengeance does not become her, and I would burn the pages where one dared ascribe such language to her, as this: **Children under the age of seven will take to trembling and will die in the arms of those who hold them.** To think that I might believe in that Apparition!" she repeated, while holding her child close to her breast, "no, no, poor little baby! That kind of devotion will never be mine; for it inspires terror and not love."[32]

That sugar was added to the vinegar and bile of Golgotha, and Mary's Ocean of Tears lost their bitterness.

Very facile effect. It sufficed to decompose the Message, by separating what is conditional from what is not, for example the public Discourse of the Secret confided to Mélanie to be published twelve years later. Now, separation is death. As long as the Secret has not been published, one could suppose it reconcilable with all sentimentalities. One allowed that it should exist. When known, it was decided to suppress it, and, as it was the heart of the Message of La Salette, that Message was as if killed, as much as anything partaking of God can be killed. How to accept in the 19th or the 20th centuries then – from Mary even! – a sort of very specific Apocalypse, an amplification or disclosure of the twenty-fourth chapter of Isaiah: *Ecce Dominus dissipabit terram*. Those things are not permitted, not even from God who has sealed his Gospel, right? and Who *must not* add one iota to

---

[32]Original footnote: *Echo of the Sacred Mountain*, by Mlle. des Brulais, Nantes, 1854.

the Revelations that his Church is the keeper of. That would exceed all measure for Christian souls, and the two witnesses of the Queen of Martyrs, the two shepherds, learnt this at their own expense.

"This place where you stand is holy ground." Haunting phrase! What must Mélanie have been feeling when she returned to La Salette after so many dolorous peregrinations! at the age of 71, on September 19, 1902, fifty-sixth anniversary of the Apparition? She hadn't much time left to suffer, and certain things, that men would not have understood, needed to be said to that extraordinary daughter of God. From all directions on her Mountain, more precious than diamond, a voice was spoken for her ears only, a Voice infinitely sweet and moaning:

"Look, Mélanie, at what they have done to our desert! Previously, you remember, one heard only the plaintive sound of the flocks and the sob of the waters. Me, Mother of God, born before the hills and fountains, I was expecting you for so long. I was waiting also for your little companion Maximin, who, twenty-seven years ago, became my companion in Paradise. For you represented to me, dear children, the entire human family. I had chosen you, and not others, to be the notaries of my Testament. Alone, among the mountains, in the vicinity of the good torrent, I heard it falling, drop by drop, the Blood of my Son. I made you see the immensity of that pain which will surprise the Saints for all Eternity. To have given such a Child, and for so little! If only you knew!... For so many centuries, I have seen a great number of empires crumble, many of which called themselves

Christian and which perished in lust or carnage. It is rare if one man out of multitudes had sometimes a feeling of compassion for his Savior. From East to West, there is a wall of red that covers half the sky, for more than one thousand years. Persecutions, wars, slavery, all the scourges of Concupiscence and Pride. And that was the time of the Saints!

Today, it is the time of lukewarm and wan demons, the time of faithless Christians, affable Christians who have a synagogue in their mind and a "butcher's shop" in their heart. There are even those disposed to spilling their blood, but very firmly re-solved not to accept misery or ignominy. Those are the *heroic ones* and there are a few of them. I tell you, the cruelest executioners of my Son have always been his friends, his brothers, his precious members in Christ, and never has God been more outraged than by Christians. You said it often, Mélanie, and here it is 56 years now and **I can no longer hold back my Son's Arm**. I have held it back, however, because I am a strong Woman, but *I will stop soon*. People must have already noticed it. I have a need to be two times stronger because He counts on me. His too gentle Heart counts on mine. He knows that I will be impla-cable: "*Maledictio matris eradicat fundamenta – In interitu vestro, ridebo et subsannabo.*[33] [34] I will break out laughing and I will mock you, when you are in the throes of death." Those words will be executed exact-ly. Derision for derision. In 1846, I gave the last warning. It is the hope and the will of the Son of God

---

[33] *Maledictio... fundamenta*: Ecclesiasticus 3:11.

[34] *In... subsannabo*: Proverbs: 1-26.

to be *avenged* by his Mother.

Chapter 8: The Sacred Heart Crowned with Thorns. Mary is the Queen of the Father

"His very gentle Heart." He is the one who said that. *Mitis Corde*. Divine excess, as always. One would say that he cannot make up his mind to punish. Mary would be there only so long as his Arm, his crushing Arm, remained suspended. A famous visionary said that Saint Joseph had too tender a heart to support the Passion and that because of that he was not a witness to it. The presentiment alone of Good Friday sufficed to make him die of compassion. Something of the sort must have ineffably existed in God. Mary's strength was needed for the holocaust, and it will be needed for the chastisement, as the Victim, so worthy of Love, seems unfit for Justice.

It is difficult to say how many devout senti-mentalities abase Mary and uncrown her. Pious Christians want a Queen crowned with roses, not thorns. Under that diadem she would cause them fear and horror. That would no longer suit the type of beauty that their miserable imaginations suppose her to possess. But the sublime Liturgy that they are ignorant of expressly wants the Savior to be crowned by his Mother,[35] but where would she get that diadem with

---

[35]Original footnote: *Missa Spineæ Coronæ D. N. J. C. Introitus.*

which to crown him if not from her own head? Was it not proper for Jesus Christ to have the most sumptuous of crowns, and what other than that of the Queen Mother's would have been worthy of her Son the King?

But I have spoken of the Heart, of that "gentle and humble" Heart that is on the altars and that all Catholics adore. It is the devotion of the Last Days – where those last days might be years or millennia. Jesus wants to triumph through the Heart, *through his Heart crowned with thorns*. For here is a mystery. One would say that the Face of the Master that intoxicated the Saints has disappeared, in direct proportion as his Heart appeared. So the sign of his Royalty, the essential sign that he possesses from his Mother, it had to come down to his Heart, and as that was a full crown, surmounted by the Cross, as is proper for Emperors, the Cross came down at the same time, planted forever in the devouring and devoured Heart that "will inherit all the earth because it is infinitely gentle."

Such is the image that one has been forced to offer for the piety of the faithful, image of childish appearance, the only one tolerable because it intends to be merely symbolic. The horrible statues representing a glorious and plastic Jesus, "in purple brocaded robe, half-exposing his chest with celestial modesty and revealing at the end of his fingers, to a Visitandine beaming with ecstasy, an enormous heart of gold"[36] crenelated with flames; those shameful and

---

[36]Original footnote: LÉON BLOY. *The Desperate Man*, chapter XLVI.

profaning effigies must, in a way, adjourn the Communion of the Saints, Remission of sins, Resurrection of the flesh, Life eternal...

No matter how much one searches, the representation of the very sacred Heart is only possible on armorial bearings or seals. It was revealed to Marguerite Marie[37] that Jesus wanted his Heart on the French standards and *dead center* amidst *fleurs de lys*. Louis the so-called Great despised that divine desire that could only be fulfilled two centuries later, in deepest obscurity, when the throne had become vacant and all the theaters of French glory having been closed, a poor prince presented himself...[38]

For the veritably theological intelligences, the *modern* devotion to the Heart of Jesus is the strongest proof that Mary must fulfill everything and that her time has come. When Christians say the so mysterious and so incomprehensible Lord's Prayer, how few know or guess that the *Adveniat Regnum tuum*[39] proclaims that Mother, with an absolute precision, and summons her so loudly that those three words have succeeded in making her descend all in tears. *It is She who is the Queen of the Father!...*

Ah! how She asks us to listen to her! *Attendite*

---

[37]Marguerite Marie: Margaret Mary Alacoque (1647-1690), a French Visitandine, mystic and inspirer of the cult of the Sacred Heart of Jesus. She was canonized as a saint in 1920.

[38]Original footnote: Léon Bloy. *The Son of Louis XVI.*

[39]*Adveniat Regnum tuum*: Latin for "Thy Kingdom come," a phrase in the Lord's prayer.

et videte si est dolor sicut dolor meus.[40] We have
waited for her for nineteen centuries. We have summoned her from every country and in every language,
morning, noon, and night, with millions of mouths.
The Apostles, Martyrs, Confessors, Virgins, Prosti-
tutes, Assassins, the Elderly on the verge of dying,
and all the little Children who knew or did not know
what they were saying, they have supplicated her to
come, and She came finally, like a poor, unhappy
soul, claiming the Seventh Day that belongs to her
and that nobody wants to give her.

She does not expressly name the Heart of Jesus, but she gives the name of Napoleon III, which is
strange and terrible. How can it be that Mary pro-
nounces the word *heart* without triggering the Deluge, the immersion, the swallowing up of Herself,
and of all the worlds in that gulf of blood and fire that
is the Heart of Christ: "The fountain left the House of
the Lord to irrigate the torrent of *thorns*," thus prophesied Joel, 600 years before the Passion.[41]

But what words are these, my God! Was she
not Herself the Heart of Christ pierced by the Lance
and torn by the Thorns, when the mad Cross was
erected? What would one believe if that was not to be
believed? One point is indisputable. We perish for not

---

[40]*Attendite... meus*: Latin for "Wait and see if there be any sorrow like unto my sorrow..." Lamentations 1:12. It is also sung in the opening lines of the Gregorian Chant beginning "*O vos omnes...*"; and at the *Tenebrae* on Good Friday.

[41]Original footnote: Joel 3:18. *Joël planus in principiis, in fine obscurior*, said Saint Jerome speaking to men who were unable to know the Sacred Heart.

having listened to it.

Chapter 9: You Knew, O My Lady of Transfixion, That I Do not Know How to Go About It...

"I will bless the houses where the image of my Heart is displayed and honored." Such is the promise. Would that this book wherein I shelter my thought be thus blessed! This book full of desire to honor the dolorous Mary:

You knew it, O My Lady of Transfixion, that I do not know how to go about it and that I have need of some help to speak of You properly. You know, O pierced Heart of the Empress of all worlds, that I would like to add to Your Glory while expanding the thought of some of my brethren. But the undertaking exceeds my power and it seems to me that I have nothing to say.

Here it is then nearly thirty years since I had boldly conceived the idea of it. One of Your friends whom You sent to me when there was no longer any voice to instruct me. He awaits the Resurrection in Your little cemetery on the Mountain. But You pursued me without respite, forcing me to speak of La Salette, all the same, in other books that were not for you alone, and finally You led by the hand, into my poor cave, one of Your most gentle sons, a very humble scholar who told me on Your behalf that, not having, according to the laws of nature, an unlimited number of years to spend on this earth, I had to comply, whether I liked it or not.

So, my Sovereign Queen, it is expedient that You assist me, for my powerlessness is great, my having, besides, a mind obfuscated by so many things that are not holy. In the universal silence, or very nearly, keep in mind that you oblige me to vociferate against the enormous injustice, without precedent, perpetrated by all Christians contemptuous of Your Tears and faithless depositories of Your most precious warnings. You give me the order to single out, like dogs that must be put down,[42] the devouring pastors of Ezekiel who are busy in such large numbers at grazing in the field themselves, and the attentive dissimulators of Your formidable Revelation.

And how many others things! If I keep quiet, who will rehabilitate Your witnesses, Your shepherds of love, Your representatives chosen from among the millions and shamefully rejected and calumniated by those same pastors who stifled them as best they could? If I grow discouraged, where is the Christian who will dare to say that it is really true that sixty years ago You came to inform us, while weeping, of the imminence of the next Deluge and that nobody wanted to believe You? You were, however, the salutary Ark that one had not even bothered to construct, as before, and wherein it is certain that more than *eight* souls could have been saved...[43]

Look now at the poor instrument that I am. A

---

[42]Original footnote: *Videte canes, videte malos operarios...* Philippians 3:2.

victim, like You, of the *conspiration of silence that* I have had for twenty-five years now, my lips so locked that I can barely eat. They alone understand me who are very close to me and heart to heart, so to speak.

But even if You lent me the voice of Jeremiah, there would be nothing for me to do as long as You had not given ears to the multitude. I am a rheum in the eye of contemporaries. The most vile enemies of God believe that they have the right to despise me, and they who declare themselves friends of the same God are the friends of my enemies. You know why, You who gave birth to the Absolute so that men might put him on the cross. But I would become an accredited ambassador if I had the power, all of a sudden, to turn water into blood, which I ask of You very humbly.

I will obey then, certain that the words I need to say will be put into my mouth, hoping for I do not know what miraculous force from You, O Mary, and filled with that enormous honor for the rest of my days.

---

[43]Original footnote: 1 Peter 3:20.

Chapter 10: Napoleon III Declares War on Mélanie

He (Pius IX) should distrust Napoleon: his heart is two-faced and when he wants to be Pope and Emperor at the same time, then God will leave him. He is that eagle that, always wanting to rise, will fall on the sword that he had wished to use to oblige the people to rise up.[44] [45]

Such is the eighth paragraph of Mélanie's Secret, confided by the Mother of God to that shepherd, on September 19, 1846. with the mission of publishing it twelve years later. While waiting, that Secret, written in Mélanie's hand by order of her bishop, to be communicated to the Pope alone, was carried to Rome in 1851 by two venerable priests who confided it, hidden and sealed, to the Sovereign Pontiff, while Maximin's remains unknown to this day.

It should be noted, to begin with, that in 1846, the future Napoleon III, whom nobody was thinking about, was locked up in the fortress of Ham, and condemned to life in prison. Even in July 1851, the Coup d'Etat and the Second Empire were still among the

---

[44]Original footnote: The last four words give the idea of a defective and amphibological construction. All the more reason, it seems, to respect them.

[45]The intent is probably this: "... the people to *help him* rise up."

things that belonged exclusively to prophets. So conclusive a fact is worth pointing out.

Did Pius IX speak? One is compelled to believe that, in one manner or another, something transpired because Louis-Napoleon, after having become emperor "by the grace of God and the nation's will," hastened to declare war on Mélanie. It was one of his first acts, and, certainly, one of the least known.

The venerated Mgr. de Bruillard, Bishop of Grenoble, who had proclaimed the Miracle, a short time before the Coup d'Etat, asked Napoleon, in November 1852, to give him a coadjutor, alleging his great age and his infirmities. The decennial president who had need of a flunky, refused the coadjutor, demanding the bishop's resignation pure and simple, in order to appoint a prelate at his discretion to the Grenoble seat, someone who did not believe in La Salette, who would bury the miracle. Thus, the Abbot Ginoulhiac, from Montpellier, vicar general of the archbishopric of Aix, and a professor of Gallican theology for many years, became the successor to Saint Hugues.

"Many a believer," said Amédée Nicolas,[46] "grew alarmed at learning who the new bishop was. But the Holy Virgin had chosen a prelate who, greatly gifted in hability, perspicacity, and prudence, familiar with the public discourse, not knowing the Secrets that caused Napoleon terror, could better conserve devotion and sanctuary by reassuring the chief of State, by affirming to him, as much as possible, and in en-

---

[46]Original footnote: *Defense and Explanation of the Secret of Mélanie of La Salette*. Nimes, 1881.

tirely good faith, that there was no hidden plot against either him or his throne. Providence is not prodigious with its miracles. As more often is the case, it makes use of, in order to achieve its ends, men who are the most mediocre in character, in their manner of being, in their qualities, even in their defects. We ourselves believe that without Mgr. Ginoulhiac's elevation to the Grenoble seat, – he who, on the other hand, was a Gallican and also pleasing to the Empire in that respect, – and without divine intervention, La Salette would have been persecuted and pursued by the Emperor. That choice of his had quite a few drawbacks to be sure; for the two witnesses it resulted in a great deal of unmerited trouble and suffering, to be sure; but it saved the most important thing, that is to say the devotion, the pilgrimage, the sanctuary, and the mountain."

It did not take long however for the new bishop to find himself in an extremely awkward situation. The Secrets, Mélanie's above all, which were said to be so menacing and which he was not yet familiar with, were like a fishbone stuck in his throat, when he needed to speak with his emperor about cormorants. "But, happily," he said, in his pastoral Instruction on November 4, 1854, "we live under a government that is sure enough of itself as not to tremble before alleged prophetic confidences made to a child..."[47] Little reassured, Napoleon III wanted to shut down the sanctuary, and it required the intervention of Jules Favre, very feared at the time, who manifested the intention of bringing the matter before the Legislative

---

[47]Original footnote: "We live under a prince who is inimical to fraud," Molière had already said [of King Louis XIV].

Body by an interpellation, in order for the government to renounce persecuting La Salette. As for Ginoulhiac, sated by so many emotions, disquieted to feel the precious crozier trembling in his hand, he decided to bring things to a conclusion once and for all by having the witnesses of Mary disappear, the "two ignorant and rough children," the "two puny instruments" who were giving His Greatness so much trouble. The surest thing would have been to have them killed, but there were too many people, too many eyes. An *expedient* was needed, no less episcopal than what Caiaphas might have come up with. The redoubtable Mélanie was exiled to England, at the end of September 1854, by an abuse of authority, primarily an iniquitous act, that one does not fail to spin as the granting of a huge favor solicited by the victim herself, the touching effect of pastoral kindness verging on weakness.

The following year, that fearsome bishop was not afraid to affirm, on the Mountain itself, that "the two children's mission was *finished* with the submission of their Secrets to the Pope, who were no longer linked anymore to the Miracle; that their acts and their words, since July 18, 1851, were completely *indifferent*; that they could go away, wander throughout the world, *become* INFIDELS to a great received grace, without the fact of the Apparition being in any way affected." At whatever price, it was a matter of demonetizing the two Witnesses.

Chapter 11: Errant Life of the Shepherdess. Cardinal Perraud, Successor to Talleyrand, Divests Her

"Why are you sad, my soul, and why give me so much trouble?" It was quite necessary though for the sad bishop to articulate that, that liturgical interrogation, before going up to the altar, the morning after, and all the other mornings after that, until the last day of his life! And when the hour of his death approached, that terrible or sweet hour of the *soul's deliverance*, with others assisting at his time of agony, he was unable to concentrate exclusively on the ritualistic phrases that open the blessed door: *Viam mandatorum tuorum cucurri.*[48] He could not do it for having had said to the saintly girl, "You're crazy!" – it was only just that he should die deprived of his reason.

One day, there will be published, for the astonishment and terror of a great many people, a monograph on the punishments inflicted on the ecclesiastical persecutors or blasphemers of La Salette. The list of them is already long.

---

[48] *Viam... concurri*: Psalms 118:32.

Mélanie could find no rest after that. After a six-year stay at the Carmel in Darlington, returned to France and arrived in Marseille, on September 28, 1860.[49] Entered, in Marseille, into a religious community to teach the alphabet to very small girls. Sent to Cephalonia and to Corfu in the Ionian Islands, in 1861 and 1862. Returned to Marseille in 1862 where she remained on a rural property until 1867 under the direction of Mgr. Petagna, Bishop of Castellammare, who had been chased from his diocese by the Piedmontese invasion and who spent his years of exile in Marseille. Departure in July 1867, for Castellammare, in Italy, not far from Naples, where she sojourned 18 years, always under the direction of Mgr. Petagna who returned to his diocese that same year, and she remained there until, and some time after, the death of that worthy and pious bishop. Around 1885, returned to France, by special permission of Leo XIII, to care for her ailing mother, at Cannes and at Cannet, until that woman's passing, then sojourned in Marseille from 1890 to 1892. Returned to Italy where she was

---

[49]Original footnote: There, she was released from the *not solemn* vows that she had made, in February 1856, at the English Carmel. By Pius IX's acknowledgement, in effect, the mission that the Holy Virgin had entrusted to her at La Salette prevented her from remaining cloistered. Soon even, that other response came from Rome, which was consulted on the subject – "*Conceal yourself as best you can.*" That was out of fear of the crowned *carbonaro*, the man with "two faces," denounced as such by the Holy Virgin herself to her confidante, with precise orders to tell Pius IX that "You should mistrust Napoleon!" – which she did by writing down her secret for the Holy Father, secret that was delivered to His Holiness, on July 18, 1851, as has already been seen. The Emperor could not stand Mélanie, feeling himself disfavorably targeted by her *Message*. Also, that prudent advice was followed up on.

stationed at Galatina this time, between Lecce and Otrante, so as to pass several years not far from her old director of conscience, Mgr. Zola, from 1892 to 1897. In 1895, trip to France, on the occasion of a sensational and scandalous trial, won, naturally, against her by Mgr. Perraud, Cardinal-Bishop d'Autun, successor to the late Talleyrand, and an academician even, who did the shepherdess the honor of depriving her, to the advantage of his episcopal mensal stipend, of an important bequest made to her for the Apostles of the Last Days. The bequest included a public chapel that the Cardinal struck with an interdiction.[50] On that subject, recrudescence of calumnies, deluge of filth. Libertinage, heresy, fraud, madness, possession! Such were the amenities of the *good press*. From September 14, 1897 to October 2, 1898, in Messina, at the Institute of Daughters of the Divine Zeal of the Heart of Jesus, to direct young aspirants during their year of novitiate. From there to Moncalieri. Then another and last return to France where she spent five years, from 1899 to 1904, at Saint-Pourçain, Diou, Cusset (Allier) and Argœuves (Somme). She returns twice to La Salette: on September 18, 1902, to spend the 56th anniversary of the Apparition; and one last time, on July 28, 1903. She had received the sacrament of Extreme Unction in Diou, during a grave illness without consequences, on January 26, 1903. Finally, in the middle of 1904, she left France definitively to establish herself in the province of Bari, Italy, where she lived incognito until her death in mid-December, known only by her new bish-

---

[50]Original footnote: Documents relative to that disgraceful affair were published, in 1898, by the publisher Chamuel, Paris. *Mélanie, Shepherdess of La Salette and the Cardinal Perraud.*

op, Mgr. Cecchini, and by a pious lady, the signora
Gianuzzi. Her last communion, on December 14, in
the Cathedral of Altamura, is her supreme Viaticum.

That continual errancy, that incessant migra-
tion, necessitated by a hostility lacking in forgiveness,
– favorable, otherwise, to the accomplishment of her
mission, – was turned against her: charged with
vagabondage, in the worst sense of the word, inter-
preted in the vilest and most heinous way. Few saints
have been so calumniated.

"I will die in Italy," she said at Diou, less than
two years before her death, "in a country I do not
know, where I know nobody, an almost savage country, but where one loves the good God; I will be
alone, on a beautiful morning, – someone will see my
shutters closed, and they will open the door forcibly,
and they will find me dead." That prophesy was real-

ized, in all its details, to the letter.[51]

The extraordinary beauty of that life was hidden, for more than sixty years, by means of a truly diabolical art, and her most precious death was not made known. Besides, at that epoch in time, who was thinking of the Shepherdess? One barely mentioned her name on the Mountain, while deploring that things had turned out badly for her. Irreproachable immolation. Maximin, dead in 1875, had been dishonored, he also, extremely studiously and in a manner that leaves nothing to be desired. Good riddance for the both of them.

The legend, solidly established since then, of the regrettable indignity of the witnesses, was turned, in the end, to God's Glory, as is ordinarily the prac-

---

[51]Original footnote: Mélanie inhabited a small house "outside the walls" in Altamura. She was *alone* there for a small period of time; and Mgr. Cecchini knew, the only person in her diocese, that she was the saint that had been confided to his safekooping. Every morning, she showed up at the cathedral, participated in the Holy Sacrifice, took communion, went to the bishop's palace to have a small cup of coffee without bread, then retired to her solitude. That was all the nourishment she took for the day. Around noon, the monseigneur, who had not yet had the occasion to *catch up* with her, that living gift who was almost without nourishment, had a regular visitor of the bishop's palace bring her her meal, which she gave to the poor. On December 15, not seeing her at the cathedral, he grew anxious and sent someone to go find her. The shutters were closed, and with no response at the door he decided to alert the civil authorities. The door was opened and the pious woman was found dead on the floor. She was entirely clothed, her clothes modestly arranged about her; her arms crossed to support her face. All one had to do was pick her up and place her religiously in the coffin...

Six months after Mélanie's death, Mgr. Cecchini had her tomb opened and found her holy body intact.

tice, – no? – by drawing the good from the bad and making the best use of contemptible instruments. The eloquence of the seminaries could make a career out of it for themselves. The unverifiable lie was taken up by all Christians, priests and laic, irreparably deceived. The Secret had become a dangerous or ridiculous revery and, for a time, the old Serpent triumphed over the Virginal Foot...!

Deus non irredetur, however: God will not be mocked. Mélanie passed away on the morning of the Octave of the Feast of the Immaculate Conception and, the day before, that year, in diverse dioceses, the Manifestation of the Miraculous Medal had been celebrated, a feast pushed back from November 27. Liturgical reminder of the Dragon vainly pursuing the Woman with the wings of an eagle who fled before him into the desert; and for that other, that abandoned moribund, the Church would have chanted the fatidic words: "POSUIT IN EA VERBA SIGNORUM SUORUM ET PRODIGIORUM SUORUM IN TERRA."[52]

Three years have passed. The buried Messenger no longer wanders the world. She is immobile and uncorrupted in a tomb that people will visit one day. But the prophecy that she brought continues its course like a river, more and more majestic, more and more redoubtable. One already hears it rumbling, and the most impavid people begin to grow afraid.

---

[52]Original footnote: *Manifestatio Immaculatæ V. M. a Sacro Numismate*. Graduale. MISSALE ROMANUM.

Chapter 12: The Priests and Mélanie's Secret

If it had been only Napoleon III, the conspiration of silence against her would not have lasted thirty-six years. Even the surprising human infirmity that transforms resentment of the most forgotten griefs into a routine; everything that could have, before the catastrophe of 1870, been used against La Salette and her Witnesses would have since dried up, with only the energy of Catholic sap demolishing the wall little by little, with each new spring. But there was this, which was not acknowledged, it being judged intolerable, and which was not wanted at any price:

The priests, ministers of my Son, the priests, by their wicked life, by their irreverence and impiety in celebrating the Holy Mysteries, by their love of money, their love of honor and pleasures, the priests have become CESSPOOLS OF IMPURITY. Yes, the priests ask for vengeance and that vengeance is suspended over their heads. Woe to the priests and the people consecrated to God, who, by their infidelity and their bad life, crucify my Son again! The sins of the people consecrated to God cry to Heaven and call down vengeance, and behold: vengeance is at their doorstep, for there is nobody to implore mercy and forgiveness for the people. THERE ARE NO MORE GENEROUS SOULS, there is no longer anyone worthy of offering the immaculate Victim

to the Eternal, in favor of the world.[53]

"Nolite tangere Christos meos... qui vos audit me audit: et qui vos spernit, me spernit."[54] You hear him, O Mother of the Verb, it is to You that that is addressed. You have dared to touch the clergy. One could think that you had the right, being their Queen, *Regina cleri*, but that means nothing and behold Your punition: We decide that You have spoken in vain.

"They do not want to take an examination of conscience," said Mélanie. *"Tu es ille vir, tu fecisti hanc rem abscondite!"* said the Holy Ghost. It's you, the guilty one! said their conscience. Whatever the crime that is committed, in whatever place in the world, that expression must be justly and rigorously applied to each one of us. The saints have always understood it in those terms. And because the priests are closest to God and, hence, the most responsible, it is natural that they should be affected first.

"You are the light of the world!" the Master said to them. There will never be a more certain affirmation. But one knows that the most candid terrestrial flame, held up to the sun, projects a shadow. In the same way, the Light of God, if it came to rise up behind the light of the world, that latter light, at that moment, would project a dark, dirty, fuliginous shadow

---

[53]Original footnote: Mélanie's Secret, 2nd paragraph. "There is this remarkable thing," observed Amédée Nicolas, thirty years ago, "that no religious community of women complained. Only the secular or regular priests cried out."

[54]*Nolite... spernit*: Latin for "Do not touch my anointed ones... he who hears you, hears me: and he who spurns you spurns me." See Psalms 104:15 and Luke 10:16.

of the most impenetrable opacity. Such must be the sensation of a humble priest who makes an *examination of conscience*. How then could he be bothered or surprised by the energy of certain phrases?

It really is a question of that! moreover. God's Word is, by essence, incontestable, indisputable, irrefragable, definitive. One is forced to receive it integrally, or to declare oneself an apostate. Now the word of Mary, it is the Word of God, as well at La Salette as in the Gospel. If she says that we are "dogs," it is eternal Wisdom speaking. If she wishes to add that priests are "cesspools of impurity," there is nothing more to do about it than to believe that things are as she says, with very humble acts of grace for the benefit of so precious a revelation and without thinking, for one minute, to *distinguish* sophistically. That word of God knows what it is saying, it knows it infinitely, and the rest of us, – we do not even know what we think.

One has spoken of "hyperbolic expressions," one has wished to save the Secret, by explaining the word *cesspool* as not meant in the absolute sense, as if God did not always speak ABSOLUTELY. Infidelity, bad living, irreverence, impiety, love of money, honor, and pleasure. Result: cesspool of impurity. What to think of a priest who would say: "That is not meant for me." Saint Francis de Sales, Saint Philip Neri, Saint Vincent de Paul, the curate d'Ars, fifty thousand others, not to mention the Martyrs, would have said while weeping: "Ah! how true it is! for our Sovereign Lady knows me, and how useless it is, my hypocrisy at every moment!" But behold! **There are no more**

generous souls. The hard truth that a man determined to give his life to God will never contest is that every priest who does not tend to Sanctity is really, rigorously, absolutely, a Judas and a piece of filth.

Just now, I cited two Texts, the first, Psalms 104: "*Nolite tangere...* Do not touch my anointed," to show the wonderful conclusion that one can draw from it. The other half of the same verse appears to be a devastating response by Mary: "*... et in prophetis meis nolite malignari...*" – and do not malign my prophets. Those persecutors of Mélanie and Maximin who had not "received their souls entirely in vain" must have trembled sometimes on reading those words in their breviaries. As for what is in the evangelical Oracle, "He who hears you, hears me, etc." doesn't anyone see that it applies primarily to Our Lady of La Salette? "Do all that he tells you to do," the Mother of Jesus had said at the wedding in Cana. "He who listens to You listens to Me, and *he who spurns You spurns Me,*" her Son replied to her, nineteen centuries later, hearing her weeping on a mountain.

Chapter 13: Mary's Immense Dignity

The incomprehension of the Fact of La Salette is a natural consequence of the incomprehension or ignorance of the Privileges – infinitely inexplicable moreover – of Mary. Speaking only of her Immaculate Conception, which is a terrifying mystery, it is to be noted that at Lourdes She does not say: "I am conceived without sin," but "*I am the Immaculate Conception.*" It is as if a mountain said: "I am the Celsitude." Mary is the only one who has the right to speak for Herself *absolutely*, just as Jesus speaks for Himself when he says: "I am the Light, the Truth, the Life." The "Clothing of the Sun,"[55] mentioned in the Apocalypse, is his clothing as an Absolute. She is next to God and so far from other creatures that one needs an effort of reason not to get confused. I dare say even, at the risk of confusing myself, that the more Reason and Faith grow, the more the Mother of God grows, and that a person becomes less and less able to delimit her, to *distinguish* her.

Ah! I know how inadequate those words are! They have at least this going for them that they are adequate to the penury of my thought. An angel itself, if one could hear its Latin without being struck by a lightning bolt of love from the first syllable it spoke – how would it explain that one can conceive of Mary without conceiving of the Trinity itself and discern

---

[55]Clothing of the Sun: Revelation 12:1.

her even a little in the dazzling sight of the great
Tenebrae?

At La Salette, She speaks *in the first person* as
God alone can speak. One noticed that in particular.
Very strong people rushed to hold up the walls of the
Church that that language, clearly, was going to pull
down; how to explain – oh! how feebly, – that all
canonical prophets have expressed themselves in that
same way and that in that encounter, their admirable
Queen is, like them, merely a megaphone, *nothing
more*. No one dares ask how the Mother of God could
have expressed herself in any other way. In the public
Discourse, it is always the Name of her Son accompa-
nying the reproaches and the threats. It has been
demonstrated to us then that She speaks, above all
and uniquely, in the capacity of the Mother of God, of
the absolute Sovereign, to the degree that that Son
who is Her Creator looks as though he can do nothing
without her permission. Try and replace the First Person by the Third, when reading, for example, "*God*
has given you six days to work, *he* has reserved the
seventh but no one wants to accord *him* it." Immediately, it becomes the parænesis of any old preacher
and whatever it is that gives a precise character to that
famous Discourse which has astonished so many
souls, – the supreme Authority, – it vanishes.

Of course Mary is not God, but she is the
Mother of God. Nothing can express her dignity however. Theologically, it is as impossible to adore her as
it is to exaggerate the cult of honor that belongs to
her. Mary's glory and her œcumenical excellence de-
fies Hyperbole. She is the Fire of Solomon that never

says: "That's enough!" She is earthly Paradise and the celestial Jerusalem. She is She to whom God has given everything. If you think of her Beauty even, it would be a derision to say that she is Beauty itself, as She infinitely surpasses that praise. If you want to exalt her Strength and her Power, you will do no better than to recognize that She is, in fact, the least of creatures, as She has been able to accomplish that unimaginable marvel of humbling herself much lower than all the abysses before She had been conceived. If you ask to die, all those dying of their own volition are in her Arms. If you ask to be born, the Milky Way will issue from her Breasts to nourish you. Whatever kind of poet you might be, capable, if I may say so, of surprising the innocent Couple under the plane trees of Paradise, you would look as though you were selling the most fetid stuff on a rigged scale, you would resemble a negro or a proprietor of poor wretches, if you should undertake – were it weeping even and on both knees! – if you should merely dream of speaking one word of her Purity which resembled the sweat of the damned from the lowest circle of hell, – the droplets of dew suspended from the silver and opal webs of pleasant spiders in the woods one summer morning.

No matter how much you pray, however much you do, you can never pay me back for the amount of trouble I have gone to for you.

If the Church Militant subsisted for another ten thousand years, and there were hundreds of councils, each one adding an inestimable gem to the adornment of that Queen, it would not do nearly as

much for her splendor as that testimony by Herself to
Herself, in the desert, in the presence of those two
poor little children.

Chapter 14: Identity of the Public Discourse and Mélanie's Secret. Eve's Lament.

Mary's expression, always identical to the Expression of the Holy Ghost that the Church calls its Spouse and which inexpressibly penetrates it, is always, *by nature*, in similes or parables. It is, above all, *iterative*, God always saying the same thing and always speaking about Himself, as I have remarked elsewhere.[56] [57] By consequence, the Secret needed to be identical to the public Discourse, and it is in this way that the common origin manifests itself. I am not proposing to interpret them. Others have tried, with more or less good fortune. But precisely because the divine Word is invariably assimilated or figurative, the prophesies are unverifiable on this side of life because, even their fulfillment is but another figuration of the future. In that sense, as in all senses, a prophet speaks forever. *Defunctus adhuc loquitur.*[58]

---

[56]Original footnote: *Salvation Through the Jews*.

[57]*Salvation Through the Jews*: Available in English translation by Sunny Lou Publishing, 2020.

[58]*Defunctus adhuc loquitur*: Latin for "The dead still speak." Hebrews 11:4.

Certain threats contained in the Secret of La Salette, such as the fall of Napoleon III, which have very visibly come to pass, – one can be sure that that catastrophe is itself prefigurative of some other great punition that no one can divine. I would even go so far as to say that that threat is not unrelated to the fall of the *first* Napoleon, for prophesies are not bound by duration, any more than by space, and it is a joy to imagine feeling them throbbing at the center of time from which they radiate throughout all worlds and *all* epochs.

Thus the necessary identity of the public Discourse and of the Secret. When Mary said to the Shepherds: **Have you not seen the ruined wheat, my children?** immediately my memory goes back to the 2nd paragraph on the priests and the people consecrated to God, the fifteen lines cited above. Same remark for the grapes that rot. The Bread and the Wine are of so significative of the Sacrifice!

The potatoes will continue to rot in the ground and at Noel there will be no more of them. Someone said to me: "The potatoes are the dead and Noel is the advent of God."[59] Now never, since the great Hebrew prophesies, had so many massacres, horrible scourges, pestilences, and famines been announced; never has the imagination been invited to see, as much as in the Secret, scenes of the earth swallowing such prodigious multitudes!

Allow me to cite here a naïvely and singularly

---

[59]Someone said to me...: See journal entry for October 8, 1914 in *On the Threshold of the Apocalypse: 1913-1915*, Leon Bloy, Sunny Lou Publishing, 2021.

lucid letter that was written to me, last year, by a lover of God:

"I dreamt that I saw a lot of people pass by whom I did not recognize. People entered and exited. There was a great coming and going. Suddenly a woman attracted my attention; she had something that touched me immensely. Everyone having departed, she said these extraordinary words to me: "*People consider me* SINLESS, I want to recount my past." Then she began to sing or to speak, for her words were like a divine song that filled me with sorrow. *It was the lament of Eve.* I woke up totally upset, totally sunk in sadness and asking myself: Where am I? It is La Salette, it is Our Lady of La Salette who spoke to me, *it is Eve who weeps*! Then the Discourse of La Salette started all over again in me, as if on its own. I understood the meaning of the words, I deciphered the phrases with ease as if I had received the key... Of all that, little remains, the lucid state has dissipated, and I no longer possess the memory of the divine thing that had taken place beside me... With her right arm, Eve nailed the Savior. – With her left arm, she un-nailed him. – 'My people' refers to the entire human race since the beginning of time. – It is Eve who is speaking while casting a glance back through the ages. – It is *she* whom the two heavy chains weigh down..."

What do you think of that new aspect of the Miracle of La Salette, of that supernatural expansion of our horizon? *Mutans Evæ nomen.* It is Mary who speaks to us, and it is Eve who speaks to us. It is the same source of life, it is the same fountain of tears. It is why her clothing, or the appearance of her clothing, is so extraordinarily symbolic.

O! that clothing! When I think of the total incomprehension of a famous writer whom our Catholics have thought precious because he had come to the Church from a very low place, and who attempts almost immediately to dishonor La Salette by ridiculing her images whose symbolism escapes him, after having ridiculed with his adjectives the Mountain itself that had overwhelmed him with its grandeur! That poor man, who thought he loved Mary, died a cruel death, a few years later, in fulfillment, I'm afraid, of the threat attached to the flank of the redoubtable Commandment: *Honora Matrem ut sis longævus super terram.*[60]

One must almost give up trying to understand the meaning of words, when it has to do with such objects. One can no longer know, for example, what a piece of clothing is. The tailor of images who made the group statues for La Salette wanted only to be the pupil of the two children and, because of that, his work has, I think, all the merit it could have. But how to translate, in marble or in bronze, the *clothing of prophesies*, a robe or a tunic of the Holy Ghost? For it is precisely *that* that the shepherds were able to see with the eyes given to them for an instant.

They said: "The Lady on fire." Could Bossuet or Saint Augustine have said it any better? One does not sculpt in fire, particularly not extra-terrestrial fire.

---

[60]*Honora... terram*: Latin for "Honor your mother that you might live long on earth." Exodus 20:12.

The face of the Lady, and Solomon's "bouquet of myrrh" hung around her neck, her Crucified son alive on her breast, were as if enveloped in an essential fire that the intensity of every volcano combined could not equal. Gold, diamonds, the most precious stones in the universe, the sun even, appeared like mud to those two children.

Persecution by Mgr. Fava. Disobedience, Criminal Infidelity of the Missionaries.

The non-existence, after sixty years, of the Order of the Apostles of the Last Days is the infinitely deplorable effect of an unprecedented disobedience, not only to the Holy Virgin who had requested its institution, but to Leo XIII who formally ordered Mgr. Fava, Bishop of Grenoble: *"to take the Rule given to Mélanie by the Very Holy Virgin and make it observed by men and women Religious who live on the Mountain of La Salette."* And Mélanie, who was received in private audience the following day had the consolation of hearing the Holy Father tell her multiple times: "You will go on the Mountain with the Rule that the Very Holy Virgin has given to you. You will make it observed by the men and women Religious." That happened on December 3, 1878.

"What happened such that nothing became of it?" she wrote, seventeen years later. "Someone I know, if he was on his death bed at that supreme moment when one says goodbye to all and sundry, to all terrestrial interests, and when his eyes see only a Judge, the scrutinizer of hearts, – he could tell us before gaining a glimpse of the other world. And he could tell us also why the orders of the Holy Father have not been followed."[61]

The constant hostility of Mgr. Fava, far more active than that of Mgr. Ginoulhiac, even though he was not goaded on by any emperor, resembles a case of diabolical possession. That inconceivable pontiff, always accompanied by his instrument of iniquity, Father Berthier, the so-called Missionaries of La Salette, harassed his victim as far as Rome – where he surprised Leo XIII with his arrogance, who did not know how to break him, – and deep into Italy where she had hoped to find a refuge, not recoiling even before that monstrous act of trying to corrupt her with *banknotes*. – "I have here several notes of one hundred francs each *for your little pleasures*," he dared to say to her. Until his dreadful death, he did not stop acting against her and hobbling her mission by all means imaginable.

She had written, on January 3, 1880: "... It is not clever of Mgr. Fava not to wish to see it my way which is completely opposite his own. My views were to make the Mountain of La Salette a new Calvary of expiation, of reparation, of immolation, of prayer, and of penance for the salvation of my dear France and the entire world. I desired that the location where the Immaculate Mary had shed so many tears should become a holy place, a model, and that one should *rigorously* observe there the holy Law of God, *the Law of Sunday*, and that neither the Fathers nor

---

[61]Original footnote: That *somebody*, properly speaking, had no *death bed*. One morning, he was found dead on the floor boards, – as Mélanie was later, – but unlike the holy woman, he was undressed, his arms were twisted, his hands clenched, his face, his *eyes*, expressing the fright of a horrible vision.

the Nuns would traffic in anything, *leaving to the seculars the trouble of selling objects of piety.*"[62]

Another lament, on September 8, 1895: "... How sad it is then to see that holy place inhabited by *unbelievers!* From the beginning, I consoled myself thinking that the Mountain where Mary had shed tears would one day be inhabited by model souls in the exact observance of the law of God, humble, charitable, devout, and zealous souls; that that holy place would become and would be the home of *penance*, of expiation, and of continual prayer for the needs of the Church and for the conversion of sinners!... I was deceived; I don't hold it against them; they understood nothing about the merciful Apparition; they do not have the religious and apostolic vocation; they are dislocated members. Would that God might enlighten them!"

The presence of the presumed Missionaries, established and prospering, for half a century, on her Mountain, crucified her. "... Those are the old missionaries," she wrote, December 29, 1903, "who have destroyed the shrine; those are the ones, alas! who have dared to *uncrown* Our Lady of Salette;[63] those are the ones, Mgr. Fava's accomplices, who have refused, against the Pope's order, to accept the Rule of

---

[62]Original footnote: *Our Lady of La Salette and Her Two Elect.* 160 letters by Mélanie. Paris, Weibel, 9, rue Clovis.

[63]Original footnote: Expulsed from the Holy Mountain, the old Missionaries took with them the strongbox, the sacred vases decorated in jewels, and even the DIADEM OF THE HOLY VIRGIN!!! One had to recur to the Pope to make them give back those riches belonging to the Shrine.

the Mother of God; those are the ones who have calumniated the so good and so humble Maximin and
who have refused to give him a morsel of bread!..." In
1901, they had asked Mélanie, in their sacristy,
"What will happen?" – "The Madonna," she replied,
"will *sweep* you away." Already Maximin, a short
time before his death, which was on March 1, 1875,
had said, while speaking of them, that "They will
come down from the Mountain and will not go back
up." Decidedly, the two Shepherds were better informed of the future than the self-styled religious, P.
Berthier, for example, who said, "After all, we are the
proprietors of the places of the Apparition. We have
purchased it by notarial instrument in due and proper
form: *nobody can dislodge us*." Adorable sweeping!
"What would be done in forgiveness," Mélanie had
also said, "will be done over their ruins."

The grief of that profanation was a martyrdom
for her. Her admirable correspondence is filled with
it, and one can honestly say that she was dead because of it after having constantly lived with it. She
could not get down on her knees, to speak to God nor
to speak to men, without that thorn piercing her heart.
"Those who stifle the truth... Material objects cloud
their intelligence... I am indignant against the spirit of
lies of the Fathers of La Salette... They are horrified
by that Secret which will lift up a corner of the veil...
Miserable religious who are not faithful!" she
groaned; "Oh! how many there are of them who will
come to the terrible Judgment of God with their hands
and their hearts empty, but their eyes full, full of desire for the goods of the earth and empty of good
works! Let us pray, pray... Our poor France is really

quite miserable and quite ill; but it is not the people who don't believe in anything who offend Divine Majesty the most; the people who belong to the demon do the work of the demon. It is the Christian souls, the Chandeliers of the Church, the Salt of the earth, who no longer do their office... *Divine Mary did not speak in order to say nothing*, nor so that *her wise warnings should go unheard...* The excuses that certain people make for not believing in the Secret are nothing but *accusations* against themselves. So as not to change one's way of life, it is much easier to say that one does not believe in the Secret, or even that it is exaggerated, so that one's evil might not seem so great; that the Very Holy Virgin could not complain about the salt of the earth, etc., etc. Those reasonings, – they should leave them for me to make, ignorant as I am! But they sound shameful to me in the mouth of people so very little educated, if not pious. What does the Holy Scripture tell us, the Old and New Testament? What does it say of the priest?... Who asked for the crucifixion of our sweet Savior?... The heresies, – by whom were they begun?... In '93, who were the first people to back the disappearance of the monarchy? etc., etc. What kind of people are they who worked against the Infallibility of the Pope?... And today, who are those who cry out against the Secret of the Virgin Mary?... The Salt of the earth!..."[64]

---

[64]Original footnote: *Our Lady of La Salette and Her Two Elect*.

Chapter 16: Mélanie's Prophetic Gifts

After what has just been read, one can easily understand the exasperation of the superb multitude of honorable ecclesiastics even, honorable principally, but contemners of the exigencies of Sanctity or Heroism.

It would not be out of place to recall here the admirable formula of the philosopher Blanc de Saint-Bonnet: "The sacred clergy make the people virtuous, the virtuous clergy make the people honest, the honest clergy make the people impious." Are we still only at the honest clergy? One could have asked himself that in 1789. Why not today? It seems to me that after so many pardons and so many crimes, the collar of maledictions must be infinitely more sumptuous. Why have we not gotten as far as outright and pure diabolism? It is quite certain, it is easily and directly observable that the very mention of, *I do not say* La Salette's, but Mélanie's Secret, or Mélanie's name simply, suffices in France to stir up the seminaries and sacristies, to bend a large number of our bishops out of shape. It pleased Mary to make use of a small shepherd to frighten powerful pastors, as if she had been a big ferocious dog before extremely timid wolves. *Et ridebit... Et subsannabit.*[65]

And then what? Is it really true then that we are the damned? If it was only a matter of an impos-

---

[65]*Et... subsannabit*: Latin for "And they shall scoff... And they shall deride." Habakkuk 1:10.

ture easily or uneasily demonstrable, there would not have been such an uproar. But it was infinitely and indisputably proven, by miracles of healing, by miracles of conversion, by miracles of prophesy that it is the Mother of God, the Mother of eternal Truth who spoke through Her Mouth, and that is what cannot be endured.[66]

Those shepherds, so obstinate in their testimonies and whose lips were unable to be "plumbed," it was not sufficient to make people believe that they were lost souls, a thousand times unworthy of the extraordinary grace that they had received, whose mission, moreover, was quite finished after the public Discourse was published; it was necessary principally to hide, at the same time as their virtues, their super-human gift of *prophesy*, which was extremely difficult.

In March 1854, – one is encouraged to note the date – Mélanie had already announced the Prussians, designating them by name, and the setting of Paris on fire. Summing up the reign of Napoleon III in three words: *Hypocrisy, Ingratitude, Treason*, the emperor was, for her, "the hypocrite, the false-hearted rogue, the cynic, the traitor, the persecutor of the Church and the Pope, dethroning God in order to crown the demon!" Not satisfied with that language, she abandoned herself to strangely significant acts.

---

[66]Original footnote: "The Gospel is closed [for additions], yes or no?" a famous Assumptionist, an enemy of prophesies and exceptional illuminations, asked me, more than 25 years ago. – "Less than you are, my dear father," I replied to him. It was not very spiritual of me, but one does what one can, with the little that one has.

It is known that she left the convent of the Providence at Corenc, in 1854, in order to be sent to England; now, after her departure, one noticed these words that she had engraved in the wood of her desk with the help of a penknife: "PRUSSIANS 1870." Still at Corenc, her teacher gave her, one day, a map of France to study. The poor child began to weep and with a single gesture *crossed out Alsace and Lorraine*. On November 28, 1870, after the disaster, she wrote to her mother: "It was 24 years ago that I knew this was going to come to pass; it was 22 years ago that I said Napoleon was a two-faced rogue, that he would ruin our poor France."

In other admirable letters, she explains what she called her "View."[67] She truly had the present and universal vision of future things "and all that in a single phrase that escapes the lips of Her who makes hell

---

[67]Original footnote: "Since the Apparition," said the Abbot Félicien Bliard, "the Shepherdess has always conserved a *clear and distinct view* of all parts of the Secret, even though it was of large scope and extremely complex; she kept the *faithful memory of all the words* of the Very Holy Virgin and the *intelligence of all that she had heard*. At the same time that the Virgin spoke to the little Shepherdess, the latter was elevated to a sublime vision in which she *saw* clearly all that was said to her. And for a quarter of a century, nothing escaped her, everything having remained faithfully engraved in her mind. Hence, that so assured knowledge that she seemed to have of the future. In the long conversations that I had with her, I was struck by the lucidity, the precision, the unshakeable firmness of her ideas. Bringing her back to the same subject, I found her always consistent in her story, without a shadow of hesitation. What's more, she is simple in words, and I found her admirable in her simplicity, candor, and prudence. When, in our meetings together, I touched on points that she had not yet revealed, I had the opportunity to admire her silence or the adroitness with which she knew how to elude every response."

tremble, the Virgin Mary." "I find it very difficult to render a thing that has no comparison... When the Holy Virgin spoke to me, I saw what she said played out; I saw the entire world, I saw the eye of the Eternal; it was a tableau in action; I saw the blood of those who were put to death and the blood of the martyrs." "... *The Holy Virgin*, IN A SINGLE WORD, *can say and convey what will take one hundred years to write about...* She uttered all the words, both of the Secret, and of the Rules, and I could divine or penetrate all that they implied. A great veil was lifted, events were uncovered before my eyes and before my imagination, all the while as Mary spoke, and before me great spaces unfolded; I saw changes in the earth, and God, unmoving in his glory, looked at the Virgin who humbled herself to speak to two dots" (Her and Maximin).[68]

In 1871, she wrote to Thiers, begging him, adjuring him, to remove the statue of Voltaire, the presence of which was, in her eyes, a frightful danger for all of France. She added that if the government did not enforce the observation of God's Commandments, the punishments already seen would be nothing in comparison to those to come. One wonders about the reception that that letter must have had on the octogenarian tightrope walker.

---

[68]Original footnote: *Our Lady of La Salette and Her Two Elect.* Mélanie's correspondence (160 letters) gives to that book an extraordinary and supernatural interest. One gets the sensation of having happily scaled the Mountain of the Prophets which is "above the terrestrial globe," according to Anne-Catherine Emmerich.

Chapter 17: Maximin's Prophetic Gifts

What man has been more vilified than Maximin? Those even who owe him everything and who let him perish in misery in their midst, – the self-styled Missionaries horribly abused their sacerdotal prestige in order to dishonor that poor boy who had given birth to them, who had clothed them and nourished them, who had given them his mountains and his sky and the Paradise in his heart, if they had wanted it![69] One knows that true Christians are the most disarmed of men, as Charity and Humility forbid them to defend themselves. The "adventuress" Mélanie, the "drunkard" Maximin, epithets that won't go away! One saw the pilgrims terrified by the eternal future of that Alexis in the tiny room of his Mother's house.

Now here is Mélanie's testimony: "Good and loyal Maximin!... I believe he has suffered a great deal and always in silence; in truth, I am filled with confusion when I see how far I have distanced myself from his life entirely hidden in God; and, if I succeed in going to Heaven, I will not touch even the heel of his feet. Often I beg him to obtain for me that generosity of the soul that would be so necessary for

---

[69]Original footnote: The old mayor of Corps, M. Barbe, has, in his hands, a note for 200 fr. (I believe) that Maximin had loaned to the Missionaries so they would not die of hunger. He held on to it after Maximin's death, paid for it to have that proof of their hard-heartedness and their avarice. M. Barbe, to whom I had written in vain to have a photograph of that document, is he still alive?

me... I thank you very much for the precious photo-graph of good Maximin, I recognized him by his bright and innocent eyes. I always think of him and all that he has suffered with extraordinary patience, with that great spirit of faith that made him see God in everything or the instruments of God in the people who made him suffer..." *Virginitate clarâ floruit*, it was said at his funeral. "No *De Profundis* over his grave, he has no need for it; let's sing *Gloria Patri* and *Te Deum*, he will bring an additional glory to the heaven he inhabits." That's Mélanie speaking again.

Maximin, he also had seen the Prussian peril a long time in advance: "*One* Italy," he wrote in 1866, "is the enemy of France like poison is the enemy of man. All the French who have blood in their veins ought to run to the assistance of Rome and beat down the Italian unification like one beats a viper. The Prussians, who have no affinity with the Italians except in their hatred of the religion of Our Lord Jesus Christ, will unite, one day, with them to punish us because we have been faithful to our right as eldest daughter of the Church to defend and protect Religion and the Papacy everywhere and in everything... I am greatly afraid lest our fervor for Italy and our complacency for Prussia will not turn against us soon, and that day is not far off."

On July 29, 1851, Maximin had spoken to an individual absolutely worthy of his trust, M. Dausse, an engineer at Grenoble, who has left his curious *Memoirs*: "When Paris will burn, there will be four kings around," which occurred to the letter. (The kings of Prussia, Bavaria, Württemberg, and Saxony.)

The same engineer recounts also that, before the Crimean War, – in 1854 – M. Michal, curate of Corenc, affirmed in the presence of Maximin that the Emperor, in a diplomatic reunion at the Tuileries, had gotten up off his throne to extend his hand to the Russian Ambassador, whence, naturally, opinion had gained ground that there would not be war with that power. "Then," continued the narrator, "Maximin comes to stand before him, arms crossed, and responds squarely: *Eh! well, me, I am telling you that there will be war with Russia!...*"

Another more surprising event. Maximin happening to be on the Mountain, on September 18 or 19, 1870, when someone mentioned Mélanie's prediction: *Paris will burn*. One of the listeners immediately gave the natural explanation for that: "That will be because of the Prussians." – "*No, no*," Maximin replied, "*it is not because of the Prussians that Paris will burn, but* ON ACCOUNT OF ITS RIFFRAFF."

On December 4, 1868, Maximin was received by the Archbishop of Paris, Mgr. Darboy, so admirably domesticated by the Emperor as one knows, Mgr. having desired to see him. The interview, as reported by Maximin, was rather long. His Greatness who, doubtless, had hoped to force the shepherd to reveal his secret to him, spoke in a manner that would deeply scandalize his listener, who had been a *Papal Zouave*, accusing the Holy Virgin of exaggerating the respect one owes to the Papacy and of having made random prophesies. – "Me too, I could make prophesies like that!" that archbishop dared say. Finally, exasperated to the point of blasphemy, he said: "At the end of the day, what kind of a discourse is that by your so-called Beautiful Lady? It is no longer French when it makes no sense... It is stupid, her discourse! And the Secret cannot be anything but stupid... No, I cannot, I, the Archbishop of Paris, authorize such a devotion!"

Maximin, humiliated by that prince of the Church who completely forgot himself in front of him, wanted that Our Lady of La Salette should have the last word. "Monseigneur," he said forcibly, "it is also true that the Holy Virgin appeared to me at La Salette and that she spoke to me, that the truth of the matter is that in 1871 – you will be *gunned down* by riffraff." Three years later, at Roquette, one assures us that the prelate, a prisoner, responded to the people who wanted to make an attempt to rescue him: "It's pointless, Maximin told me that I would be *gunned down*."

The famous lawyer of the La Salette, Amédée Nicolas, recounts the following incident which he was witness to on the Mountain, in August 1871: "A learned professor of theology and his friend, a curate from a large city, had come to La Salette, with a dozen of objections prepared and studied in advance, to propose to Maximin when he was leaving his stall in order to come, on the request of the pilgrims (who preferred him to the missionaries), to recount the story of the Miracle. When Maximin was done speaking to the pilgrims, the professor put forward the first objection. Maximin said only this: "Pass on to the second." Similarly for the second, third, and fourth. At the fifth, he responded in several words. That re-

sponse immediately made the first five objections collapse, and that collapsing brought down with it the
seven remaining objections. Seeing this, the professor
and curate told us, for we were standing beside them:
"This young man is always in his mission; he is assisted by the Holy Virgin, today as on the first days; it
is evident to us. No theologian, were he the most
knowledgeable theologian in the world, could have
done what he just did, it was a *tour de force*. All that
is certainly superhuman. He has proven the Miracle to
us better than the strongest demonstrations could have
done."[70]

Maximin's life has been one of the bumpiest.
After having spent several years in a seminary, he became a soldier, then a student of medicine. But he
failed in everything he tried his hand at and saw himself reduced to assisting laborers in order to live, to
gain his daily bread.

Finding himself in Paris in the greatest state of
destitution, he pawned a piece of clothing at the Mont-de-Piété. One day, at the end of his resources, and
no longer having anything to eat, he entered Saint-
Sulpice and was kneeling before the altar of the Holy
Virgin. "I'm really hungry," he said, "my good Mother, are you going to let me die of hunger then? And
yet, everything you have commanded of me, I have
done it. I have passed on to all your people the grave
and solemn warnings that you came to bring. It will
not be long before I collapse for inanition. If you do
not wish to pull me up out of the misery where I find

---

[70]Original footnote: *Defense and Explanation of Mélanie's Secret.*
Nîmes, 1881.

myself, then I will go address myself to your spouse, Saint Joseph, who surely will have pity on me!"

Weak on account of a prolonged fast, he soon dozes off. A man whom he does not know wakes him, invites him to follow him into a restaurant, and has him served with a copious meal. When he has regained his strength, the unknown person pays the maître d' and tells Maximin to go to the Mont-de-Piété to get back the habit he had pawned. He adds that he will find in the pocket of that habit a document which will give him shelter from misery. Then he disappears. Maximin never found out who that man was. How did the unknown man know that he had pawned his habit at the Mont-de-Piété? How did he know that he had in the pocket of his habit a document assuring Maximin's future? The latter, unable naturally to explain so extraordinary a thing, has always believed that that stranger was Saint Joseph.

Docilely, Maximin betakes himself to the Mont-de-Piété and indeed finds in the pocket of his habit a *testament* that a charitable person had made in his favor. By that testament, someone offered to receive him into a family, and he was left fifteen thousand francs to provide for his needs. How did that testament find its way into the pocket of Maximin's habit? He never knew. But what was that document worth? Maximin showed it to a notary who found it to be in proper form and made the necessary haste to execute it. He paid him then the fifteen thousand francs, and Maximin invested them in a business having to do with animals, which foundered.[71] His mission required that he live and die in indigence. How many other stories of the same kind!

I hear the immense choir of sacristine voices from here: "The *sanctity* of Mélanie and Maximin, in their capacity as *prophets*! But, sir, that turns all our ideas upside-down! You cannot make us believe that so many good Christians, so many venerable pastors, for so many years, knew nothing about it and that a contrary legend was able to be established! That supposition is unreasonable." That reminds me of the beautiful comment made by a traveling salesman when someone was speaking to him about the Papal Palace in Avignon: "What a nice joke! If there had been popes in Avignon, *we would have known about it!*" Eh! clearly. There is some knowledge of it even, but it is a rule without exception that, in order to know, one must instruct oneself with a child's candor and the humble goodwill of those other *pastors* to whom the angels of Noel formerly promised "peace on earth." "*Invenietis* infantes, *pannis* involutos *et* positos *in præsepio*."[72] [73]

---

[71]Original footnote: *Mélanie, Shepherdess of La Salette and the Cardinal Perraud.* Paris, Chamuel, 1898.

[72]Original footnote: I ask pardon for the liberty that I seem to take with the text of Saint Luke, but it is impossible for me not to think of Noel when I think of the two sublime, poor children on their Mountain.

[73]*Invenietis... præsepio*: Latin for "And this shall be a sign unto you; Ye shall find the *babes* wrapped in swaddling clothes, lying in a manger." As for Bloy's footnote (see preceding), he changed the quote from singular to plural. See Luke 2:12 for the original.

Ignorance, culpable or not, of the greatest event in modern history and of immediate consequence, to wit the eminent sanctity of the two Witnesses, will not prevent the latter from continuing their mission from the bottom of their graves and which the Church, one day, perhaps will call miraculous. *Defuncti adhuc loquuntur.* That ignorance, monstrous in all cases, will not prevent a few souls from having hope any more than hundreds of millions of arms from being twisted by despair, at the appointed hour.

One recalls that Mélanie's Secret had been published in 1879, with the *imprimatur* by Mgr. Zola, Bishop of Lecce. That Latin phrase,[74] significative of so much bitterness, tribulations, and battles for the saintly girl, stayed strangely and deeply in her memory.

"As no one wants anything to do with the Message, the cure for our evils, divine Justice will avenge the ingratitude of men and *will give* an IMPRIMATUR to the scourges announced by the Queen of Angels"!!! Thus did the Shepherdess of La Salette express herself on May 23, 1904.

---

[74]Latin phrase: scil., *imprimatur*, which means "let it be printed." A declaration or mark of approval, by a censor in the Catholic church, for publication,.

Chapter 18: The Bishops of Grenoble at Soissons

Oh! what a book to write! To demonstrate methodically the absolute identity of the public Discourse with Mélanie's Secret and the eternal impossibility of separating them, in such manner as to shine light on the deep and magnificent unity of the Revelation of September 19. Of course, in the things that treat of God, perfect evidence is not to be hoped for, but is it too much to ask to consider the following at least: that the Discourse and the Secret swap positions continually, like a face in a mirror, like the Invisible in the Visible, like the Creator in his Creature?...

It is inconceivable that such a work hasn't been written yet. I have thought about it seriously, and I will do it maybe one day, God assisting. But, not to mention my insufficiency which is frightful, it is certain that such a study would seem like a monstrous hors-d'œuvre. Keeping in mind that it would need the intervention of an Isaiah, "the seer of future things for the consolation of those who weep on the Mountain";[75] Isaiah, in his 24th chapter where he speaks of the "*Secret* of God, so redoubtable to whomever is the depository of it, and of the prevarication of transgressors." That chapter, written twenty-six centuries ago, is an echo marvelously in advance of Mélanie's Secret, and the public Discourse on La Salette reverberates that echo, completely impercepti-

---

[75]Original footnote: Ecclesiasticus 48:27.

ble without it. It is the meaning of the last phrase by
Mary: **Pass it on to all my people**. Pass it on, at least,
to the generations of twenty-six centuries.

Once again, I do not take on the responsibility
of that immense labor of interpretation that would demand, I fear, the miraculously illuminated intelligence of a saint. But it is something to feel that colossal concordance and to warn people about it, the humble people who seek God amorously.[76]

The reality of Mélanie's Secret is undeniable,
as even those who **attach little importance to it** are
forced, each day, on the exact spot where the Holy
Virgin manifested herself, to admit that She had given
a secret to each of the two shepherds, and to allege, at
the same time, one knows not what in an effort to explain their inexcusable incredulity.

It is oppressive to think that since Mélanie's
Secret has been made known, that is to say for forty
years now, not a *single* pontiff has been met on the
episcopal seat of Grenoble who was capable of feel-

---

[76]Original footnote: Where would such a work not lead? It would
require a long study of the Holy Books in order to know how
difficult it is to find one's way in the ever virgin forest of
Assimilations. Example: The Discourse speaks of **nuts** that **will
go bad**. Now, the Vulgate mentions them exactly *six* times, five
times in *Exodus*, where they assume the form of the candle-rings
on the Tabernacle's Chandelier, and one time only in *Song of
Songs*, when it is a question of Mary who descends into her
garden: "Who is She who comes, rising like the dawn, beautiful
like the moon, elect like the sun, terrible like the army of hosts
lined up? I have descended into the garden of nuts, in order to
see the fruit of the valleys, and to see if the vines are in flower
and if the pomegranates are germinating." Song of Songs, 4:9-
10. This Text, read at La Salette, by an attentive Christian, will
seem a bit fearsome to the listener.

ing the inexpressible honor of being the head of a diocese where the Mother of God has deigned to prophesy Herself; confiding, for all the earth, in two children of that incredibly privileged diocese, the unprecedented Message of divine Impatience at its tether end, and the announcement, – conditional, doubtless, but for how long? – of the last Deluge!

I have learnt with stupefaction, – persuaded that certain behavior was no longer tenable – that the present titular, Mgr. Henry, most recently, at La Salette even, has publicly expressed doubts about the Secret, *demanding proof!!!* of explicit and formal affirmations from the Court of Rome, as if the approbations, the ORDERS even, of Pius IX and Leo XIII were not sufficient![77] How shameful! It is absolutely impossible for Mgr. Henry to be unfamiliar with that entire history, that is to say the terrible disobedience of his predecessor Fava whose demise ought to make him shudder. He cannot *not* know about the constant lie put forward by opponents and their diabolical spirit of calumny against a *stigmatized* person whom he will be forced, one day, – should God let him live – to make all his priests honor. He is therefore in a state of blatant prevarication, *sciens et prudens*, a knowing and declared enemy of the Mother of God. His only excuse, – how miserable! – would be pusillanimity, invincible indecision, chronic irresolution, sempiternal dawdling.

---

[77] Original footnote: That was on July 14, 1907. Mgr. Henry spoke, from the cathedra of La Salette, to more than a thousand pilgrims: "You have come in crowds... on this Holiday both national and MARIAN!!!?" he said to them, signifying thus a sort of festival on equal footing for both the assassins of the Bastille and Our Lady of Seven Sorrows.

The same day of his taking possession, that Bishop of Grenoble – of Grenoble! – said this: "At this time, the difficulty is not doing one's duty, but knowing what it is." Words that echo the Bishop of Orleans on August 26, 1902, at Our Lady of Délivrande:[78] "It is always easy to do one's duty, it is more difficult to know what it is." An analogy will make the enormity of that backtracking understood.

In March 1814, France, trampled on, violated, devoured by six hundred thousand foreign troops, was about to be delivered by Napoleon. A divine strategy, that only the greatest marvels since Hannibal can be compared to, was going to save the day. The atro-

---

"... Monseigneur exposes then the Fact of La Salette... *He makes an effort to distinguish the Public message from the Secret message.* The children received the order and the mission to 'pass the first on to all Mary's people,' that is to say to the entire world (which hatred did not allow); the second was destined only for the Shepherds themselves (episcopal refutation of the Holy Virgin who had said to Mélanie: **You will be able to publish it in 1858**) who, perfectly aware of that necessary (?) distinction and always ready to retell the Beautiful Lady's Discourse, consented, after five years of silence and absolute reserve, to reveal their Secrets to the Pope alone. About which, His Greatness warns the faithful against all fantastical writings and commentaries that circulate and claim to reproduce 'Mélanie's Secret.' (*Reproduction* blessed by Pius IX, approved by many bishops, encouraged, for 25 years, by the silence of Leo XIII. But that does not suffice any Grenoble bishop.) Once again, the Pope alone was made aware of that secret in 1851; and *nothing proves (!!!)* that the recently published elucubrations are conformant with the earlier text... The Bishop of Grenoble waits for Rome to speak. (Always the same tactic of the Devil. If Rome spoke, one would respond like Fava: 'Prove to me that you are right.')" – *Annals of Our Lady of La Salette, August 1907.*

[78]Our Lady of Délivrande: In reference to the basilica of Notre-Dame de la Délivrande, in Douvres-la-Délivrande, Normandy.

cious Blücher was between a rock and a hard place when that man of Jena and Montmirail was about to crush his sixty thousand Prussians. By God's will, a single man's lack of will turned what would have been the most beautiful of all victories into a rout.

That general Moreau, that disappointing capitulator of Soissons, was not however a bought man, nor a soldier who lacked courage, – no one has said so at any rate. He was simply a mediocre man, an imbecile who lacked resolution and self-respect, who thought that there was something better to do as an officer than to obey, and whose vile prudence was a death warrant for multitudes. That man also asked himself where his duty lay, forgetting the orders that he had merely to carry out to the letter, in terms of Ordonnance in the service of places of war, in other words "by employing all means of defense, *by turning a deaf ear to the new communiqués issued by the enemy, and by resisting both its insinuations and its attacks*." The imperial decree of 1811 contained this quasi prophetic instruction: "The commanding officer of a place of war must remember that he defends one of the boulevards of our kingdom, a support point for our armies, and that his surrender, *advanced or delayed by one single day*, can be of the greatest consequence for the defense of the State and the safety of the army." "When a soldier begins to question *where his duty lies*," the excellent historian Henry Houssaye said, in this respect, "he is dangerously close to pursuing his own interests."

La Salette is probably the last boulevard of Christianity, and here we are forty years since that fortress capitulated!

Chapter 19: Profitable Sacerdocy. Vanity of Works in Full Disobedience. Punishments. Darkness

The dirty secret of sacerdotal hostility against Mélanie's Secret is that it would mean, by accepting it, to renounce *profitable sacerdocy*, to say goodbye to casual offerings, tariffs, *classes*, the execrable tinkling sound of money in churches. Supposing even a clergy of an admirable purity of mores, where is the priest who would dare declare any degree of horror, of whatever sort, for that traffic of the "dove sellers" and the "money changers" in the House of the Lord, thus transformed into a "cave of brigands"? For such is the precision of the evangelical Text. Where is the parish curate who would dare give first place to the Friends of God, to the barefoot beggars who are so dear to it, while sending the rich, with their padded prie-Dieus, to the back of the church, as faraway as possible from the altar? *Sancta sanctis, non canibus.* That audacious man would soon be denounced by all his clerical colleagues and severely called out by the diocesan authority.[79]

---

[79]Original footnote: The padded prie-Dieus. Prevarication denounced by Saint James, 2:2-4.

It is really a matter of cherishing poverty and humiliation! No one is bound by the *letter* of the Gospel. Maybe it was suitable for the first Apostles or to some dusty monks of the eleventh century; it means nothing to Sulpicians whom the *spirit* enlivens and who are forced to go out into the world. Then again, it is always easy to turn into a *counsel* of perfection the truly excessive *precept* of hating everything, of leaving everything behind, of selling everything in order to become the disciples and companions of Jesus Christ.

The Holy Virgin having spoken strongly about the clergy: in the Discourse, to begin with, in a very shrouded manner; then in the Secret, explicitly.[80] It was quite necessary that the "sewer" protested – in the manner of sewers, by exhaling asphyxia. The Christian world is no longer be able to breathe. By 1846 already, all was lost. A unique remedy, supernatural, was brought down from on high by the Mother of God who was weeping. The "Father of the family, planter of the Vine, and constructor of the Tower," could he really believe that that would do anything? Could eternal Wisdom say to itself: *Verebuntur Matrem meam*? The stench from the cesspool suffocated that Revelation so perfectly that the good priests themselves acknowledge their ignorance of the cure.

---

[80]Original footnote: **The heads, the leaders of God's people, have neglected prayer and penance**... 5th paragraph of the Secret. **Those who lead the ox carts**, it is said in the Discourse. That comparison will strike people habituated to the mystery of concordances. "Those who lead the ox carts" are they not, clearly, the priests who **do not know how to speak without mentioning the name of my Son?** *Pater mi, pater mi, currus Israel, auriga ejus.* IV Kings 2:12, 13:14.

From then on, how to describe sufficiently the vanity of works accomplished in full disobedience?

"One will go to La Salette," an excellent priest wrote, "one will go to Lourdes, to Paray-le-Monial, to Rome, to Jerusalem, etc., chanting: 'Save Rome and France!'" That's all one does for thirty some odd years now. One will invent pilgrimages of men and even of priests. One will organize congresses for the Holy Virgin, Eucharistic congresses, leagues of *Ave Maria*, novenas, etc. And the sky will continue to be made of bronze. All that will be of perfect insignificance for appeasing an irritated God because, at the end of the day, *one lives as one pleases* and, so as not to hear the reproaches of his Mother, one tramples on her Message.

Let's let Mélanie speak: "... It seems to me that for a long time now, I tap on the bell lightly to warn humans *that we are heading for the sad and lugubrious events of the reign of the Antichrist.* 'Is not faith dying?' – 'No,' someone will tell us. – 'If faith is not dead, let's see its works, for faith walks hand in hand with works.' – 'But,' someone else will respond, 'one makes pilgrimages; a large number of good works are performed.' – 'So it is, French people are naturally attracted to *exterior* acts; but if those pilgrimages were done in expiation, to deflect God's just anger, to beg his pardon, etc.,... have people put on burlap sacks and covered themselves in ashes in sincere penance?' – 'No!' – 'Has one at least left behind those diabolical and indecent modes of behavior, etc.? ' – 'No, nothing of the sort! Right after having visited Holy Places and Sanctuaries, one frequents the theater, just as before...' One could count the elect, fundamentally Christian souls, on the fingers of one hand; the others cannot be counted. *Apostasy is more or less endemic*. The Antichrist will not have a lot of trouble establishing his reign in Europe; those who, at the present hour, govern France, prepare it for him without meeting any obstacles. Poor France!... While waiting, it laughs, it amuses itself, because it does not believe in a better life; because it has no faith, but simply the *vanity of faith*, by feigning religion, by having itself written down as the DIRECTRESS OR ZEALOTRESS OR PRESIDENTRESS of such and such a confraternity." That letter is dated November 28, 1887.

One year earlier, when many journalists were growing restless, she had already written this: "... It is pointless to take the trouble to try and guess *what the prince who mounts the throne of France will be like*. If one did not know the Secret, one would be pardonable: **For a time, God will no longer remember France or Italy**. One has revolted against God and his mild law: we will be governed by an iron rod, and strict and hateful laws will be imposed on us. Those who govern us are merely instruments in the hands of the Almighty. As the wicked make advances on Catholic terrain, we will have the cowardice to retreat... We will submit to all the exigencies of the enemies of God and souls. Some protest, you say? Yes, some protest! It does not cost much! The first Christians protested with their blood, with their lives. Come on! We are merely the *shadows of Christians*, we fear the punishments of men more than the pain of Hell. Do you believe that the good God will give

France a king before having justly and severely chastised it? And afterwards, will we be counted among the living? *All intrigues of certain claimants to the French throne are but child's play.*[81]

"... One thing causes me the greatest sadness. It's the *diabolical* habit of procuring aid for the victims of an earthquake, or any other catastrophe, by throwing dances, and theatrical representations. *I cannot accept that one dares resort to an evil in order to effect a good.*[82] Oh! the blindness of Godless men! And those acting in that way call themselves Christians! I have no doubt about it, we are drawing close to a great war, that is to say, *to the advent of the man of perdition, of the Antichrist.* Well do I know that people do not consent to recognize a truth that frightens them, but which is nonetheless true. *Our generation marches straight towards the Antichrist* WHOM IT MUST GO OUT TO MEET; and the indifferent refuse to believe and the impious to rail. That's how it is. Woe! woe! woe!

"... I am frozen with fear upon seeing the rage of hell and men, including infernal (sic) women; fire and blood will have a field day. What massacres! What ghastly tortures! Oh! those women are terrible! The poor priests who fall into their hands!...

"**The Church will undergo a dreadful crisis**, ... Explusion of curates from their presbyteries, of

---

[81]Original footnote: It is [perhaps] pointless to note the *actual date* of this page, written more than twenty years ago.

[82]Original footnote: Léon Bloy. My Journal. "Letter on the fire at the Charity Bazaar."

bishops from their palaces, the seer pursued; closure and confiscation of churches; massacres of clergy worse than what happened under the Reign of Terror. Many will be killed for personal vengeance. Those who falter will not be spared: the plan of Free Masons is to make those who are consecrated sin before killing them! I saw that those violent deaths were, in very large part, *altogether different from martyrdom*; that that was the fulfillment, in all its horror, of the word 'Woe!' as written in Scripture... You do not want the Message of mercy, you push away the hand extended to you; there is no longer anything you can do about it: **God will leave men to themselves... that will be the time of darkness**."[83]

---

[83]Original footnote: A tradition has it that France, after a long period of iniquity, at a time that resembles our own, will wake up one morning without seeing the sun rise. For many days, it will remain in darkness in the midst of which specters, come from Hell, will come to torment the living. There exists an analogous prediction by the Venerable Anna-Marie Taïgi, passed away in 1837.

Chapter 20: The Woman Bent Over for 18 Years, Image of La Salette. Mary Speaks. Jesus no Longer Speaks then? The Immaculate Conception Crowned by Thorns, *Stigmatized*. Lourdes and La Salette

There is in Saint Luke, the evangelist of Mary, a story that will never be able to be read with enough attention and respect:

"Jesus was teaching in the synagogue on a day of the Sabbath. A woman approached who had for eighteen years been possessed by a spirit of infirmity. She was bent over and absolutely could not look up. Jesus, on seeing her, called out to her and said: 'Woman, you are delivered of your infirmity.' And he put his hands on her. She immediately straightened up and glorified God."

I will never grow tired of saying that the Gospel, as well as the Old Testament, is essentially parabolic, figurative, prophetic, the Holy Ghost never having spoken in any other way. So who is that woman, possessed for eighteen years, by a spirit of infirmity? I see only Mary to identify such a figure.

O Mary! My Lady of Compassion! What have you come here to do?

It is, in effect, the day of the Sabbath, Saturday, the eve of your Sorrows.[84] Behold precisely *eighteen* centuries already that you are bent over and mute, the Spouse who happily possesses you being himself, although God, – by impenetrable mystery – a Spirit of infirmity and curvature, until the marvelous hour when He will instruct us in everything. For *eighteen* centuries you have kept silent, after having spoken only six times[85] in the first four books of the Gospel! At La Salette finally, and for the seventh time, you speak with so sovereign an authority that

---

[84] Original footnote: One knows that the Apparition took place on a Saturday, September 19, 1846, the eve, that year, of the feast of Our Lady of Seven Sorrows, and at the hour of first vespers. It was also the last day of the Ember Days of September. That very morning, the great ferial Liturgy had included these words from Leviticus: "It is the very celebrated day of Expiations and it will be called Holy... it is the day of propitiation for reconciling yourself with the Lord. Every soul that will not be afflicted on this day shall perish." And soon thereafter, in the Gospel, O! the story of the woman bent over for eighteen years, made to stand up straight by Jesus, and glorifying God!!! *Roman missal.*

[85] Original footnote: Four times in Saint Luke, two times in Saint John: Each time, She mounts one of the Six degrees of the ivory Throne sat on by that eternal Solomon, to the right of whom her place is marked, in the middle of the Twelve Lion Cubs of the Apostolate. II Par. 9:18-19.

afterwards there can be nothing else for it but universal Judgment and combustion of worlds. You speak thus because Jesus has delivered you, that is what I read in the Gospel, and you glorify God as no one else could do. However, it is not yet your victory, for behold the "leader of the synagogue" followed by many priests who are all of them indignant that Jesus should have performed a miracle on the day of the Sabbath, that is to say that he has allowed you to be their judge. It is surprising, that leader of "hypocrites" who uses your own words, O Mother of the Word, in order to condemn your Son while despising you: "There are six days for work, he said..." The Holy Ghost is so bound to its Spouse that if one knew how to read one would find La Salette written on every page of the Gospel.

The Revelation of La Salette, envisaged like a rupture of eighteen centuries of silence, offers, at the same time, both consolation and terror. And I am not even thinking here about the *Message*, that is to say the menaces and the promises. I have simply before my eyes the exceptional fact of the Holy Virgin speaking *with authority* in the Church.

I said that that fact is consoling, by reason of the character of She who speaks, as the Church invokes her by the name of *Consolatrix* and, also, because it is a sort of fulfillment, *under our very eyes*, of the Third Word of the dying Jesus. But it is, at the same time, terrible because of the silence of that same Jesus who seems to be implicated. Jesus and Mary do not speak together. When Jesus begins his Predication, Mary plunges into silence and, if She breaks that silence today – is it to say that Jesus will no longer speak? That there, it seems to me, is one of the most obscure sides of the La Salette and one of the least explored, probably on account of the immense fear that one meets with. Some ascetic writers such as the holy Bishop of Lausanne, Amadée, and principally, in the seventeenth century, the Venerable Grignion de Montfort, have affirmed that Mary's Kingdom is reserved for the last days, which would give one to suppose that with our Mary having finally spoken as Sovereign, Jesus will refrain from speaking except to make known his redoubtable ESURIVI, *I was hungry*,[86] which ought put an end to everything...

I write this on the day of the Assumption. Others see Mary in glory, I see her in ignominy. Try as I may, I cannot imagine the Mother of the sorrowful Christ in the gentle light of Lourdes. I just can't see it. I do not see the attraction for an Immaculate Conception crowned with roses, white and blue, surrounded by sweet music and perfumes. I am too sullied, too far from innocence, too near the goats, too needy for forgiveness.[87]

---

[86] Original footnote: Matthew 25:35, and 25:42.

[87] Original footnote: Some will not fail to say that I am an enemy of Lourdes. Alas! I would easily give my life, God only knows, and I would consent to submit to hideous torments rather than decry a sanctuary where Mary has manifested herself by her prodigies. I know, moreover, that the miracle of Lourdes has been a *continuation* of the miracle of La Salette, like a rainbow following a storm, and I hope one day to demonstrate it much better than by that image. But it is the right of every Christian to have a preference, a particular attraction. I think even that it is his duty to follow it, God thus pointing out his way to him.

What I need is an Immaculate Conception crowned with thorns, My Lady of La Salette, the Immaculate Conception *stigmatized*, infinitely bloody and pale, and desolate, and terrible, with her tears and her chains, in the somber dress of a "Dominatrix of nations, made into a widow, crouching in solitude"; the Virgin of the Swords, such as all the Middle Ages saw it: a Medusa of innocence, and of sorrow, who transformed those who saw her weeping into the stones of the cathedral.

The priests are for her what they are for God and the Church. Each one of them represents Jesus Christ and I see her very clearly on her knees before them as she was on her knees before her Son, when he came to ask her humbly for the permission to suffer.[88]

"I beg you," she said to them, "my very dear children, do not despise my Message. It is my last effort to save the flock that you are the pastors of and for whom you will be held to a strict accounting. If

---

"I ask for two things," I wrote, several years ago: "1st that a Christian in good health go to Lourdes to *obtain* the benefit of a malady; 2nd that another Christian, rich, healed at Lourdes by the indubitable miracle, return home to give away his possessions to the poor. As long as I have not seen these two things, I believe that the Enemy has wanted to profane, by Playacting, Mediocrity, and Avarice, the unique place where it was AFFIRMED, of all the Mysteries the one he abhors the most: the Immaculate Conception."

The Virgin of Lourdes has prescribed *penance*, someone will object. One knows what penance is to the people of the world.

[88]Original footnote: Mary of Jesus of Agreda.

you do not tell them that I came and that I wept over them bitterly, if you do not repeat *all* my words, which can teach them about him, how will any of you be saved? All that I said to my two witnesses, all that I have revealed to them to pass on to all my people is infinitely precious and salutary, and you cannot make a choice without wounding me in the eye, without piercing your souls...

"You who have received so much from my Son, to the degree that you hold his divine place, you who ought to be so holy! how can you stand there and not weep with me and beat your chests? How is it you dare to mock my warnings and prevent others from believing?... I have given one Rule. What have you done with it? Two popes have in vain wanted to make it a practice. My dear Apostles of the Last Days, my dearly beloved children, where are they? I chose them myself, hand picked them with care, like grains of wheat for the Bread of Angels. Some are very near to you. If I name them, immediately you will make them suffer... By the most fearsome Name of your Master whom you force to come down each day, *I beg you to have fear...*"

"What needs to be done then?" a priest asked Mélanie; he fashioned himself "a bit like Saint Thomas." "The penance of the Ninevites," she responded. "Oh! in that case, no, we do not have the faith, nor the strength, nowadays." "Eh! well, you will have punishments harder than the penance and, lacking the strength, you will renounce God."

"*It's done!*" said the voices from Below which are in the process of rising and which cannot be heard yet.

Chapter 21: Profanation of Sunday

Everyone knows that blasphemy and the refusal to sanctify Sunday were the two great reproaches made by La Salette, the two mortal accusations, **the two things that weighed down so heavily the Arm of my Son**. But even then, we will mention it in passing, the agreement of the public Discourse with the Secret is flagrant, for it is said in the latter that **even the people consecrated to God... will assume the spirit of bad angels, and abomination will be seen in holy places**, which necessarily implicates the absolute for the profanations and supposed repudiations of those two terrible crimes.

Once again, I have not undertaken to explain those deep and divine similarities, nor even to show them, for the intended execution of which more light is needed, I suppose, than God habitually accords writers who are not ecclesiastical writers. But consider this, much to the point, a small and very posthumous book by Paul Verlaine, *Voyage in France by a Frenchman*, which contains a nice protestation by that great, unfortunate poet against work on Sunday.

Ah! I am fully aware that he is not, he neither, an authority. Far from it! One will realize eventually, in the pious world, that Paul Verlaine wrote the most beautiful [Catholic] verse there is, in praise of "his Mother Mary," to the glory of Penance and the Holy Sacrament, and that he is, in reality, the only Catholic

poet since the inspired ones of the great Hymnary; but
it will take time. Another half a century for the elite
among our seminaries, and one hundred years at least
for one third of the others, from the time of François
Coppée's death, which does not appear impending.
All the same, "poor Lélian," towards 1880, presented
in prose that original and great idea that the law of
work, ordinarily regarded as a malediction, is, on the
contrary, the "last and only consoling memory of
earthly Paradise." On reading that, I believe I have
seen the so-well guarded Gate open up before me just
a crack.

Ah! how fine that is! Thus God, totally upset
as he is against man and condemning him to lose everything, would have employed this adorable ruse to
flagellate with Hope, to inflict on him like a chastisement what ought to be his recomfort and to tie him up
rudely by a chain of Dilection! Caught up in his own,
much stronger, footlocks, the lamentable Verlaine –
he saw that! He saw, or he saw briefly, that if a lazy
man effected the terrifying act of severing the last
mooring rope, that perverse worker, who is only
courageous on Sundays because he can brave an invisible master, – he renews, unbeknownst to himself,
being a frightening beast, the original Crime and loses
again the Garden of Voluptuousness, every time, for
himself and for many others. Adam and Eve must
have, in a way that we are ignorant of, despised the
Seventh Day and **worked on Sunday all through
summer**, or **did not go to Mass except to mock religion**, or, **during Lent, went to the butcher's shop
like dogs**, for divine words are always certain and
identical, upstream as well as downstream of their

eternal course.

The sanctification of Sunday, it is the sanctification of work, and work, not sanctified in that way, is so accursed that the *apparent* solidity of private homes or public monuments, the construction of which were done on Sunday, is a problem. The Secret announces immense problems, that no prophet has ever previously announced, of such terrible or universal proportions. **The earth will be struck by all sorts of wounds. The mountains and all nature will tremble with fear.** The prodromes, besides, are manifesting themselves. Public newspapers, prodromes themselves of the world's dementia, tell of, every day, without anyone understanding, the most alarming catastrophes: earthquakes or volcanoes destroying large cities, entire countries; explosions, fire, innumerable accidents of every sort, procured by scientific or industrial assistance, in the service of Disobedience or Pride. Not to mention the continual homicides, more and more atrocious, which are a prelude, before our eyes, to merciless massacres. Yesterday, a train full of travelers jumped into the Loire... The hour is about to sound when catastrophes will occur *one after the other*, when there will be nothing but catastrophes. With each turn of that wheel of torture, the movement of which is accelerating, grave individuals immediately look for "responsibilities," in the hope, one might say, of augmenting the evil, by reducing some unprotected mercenary to despair.

Ah! how miserable we are! The responsibility lies with each one of us! The word *chastisement* revolts our pride. We need natural causes, scientific explanations, where God does not enter into the picture... That work has been done well, however! The materials were excellent, and one had the workers. There was nothing to find fault with in those bases of hard rock, capable of sustaining a mountain, and that iron framework with its beams, its bolts, its rivets, which was, what do I know? beyond praise... But here's the thing. That work was done on a Sunday, very probably, and the workers – one only, perhaps – had had to put **the Name of my Son in the midst of it**. No more was needed. Such is the explanation of the Mother of God.

I have reserved the Seventh Day for myself. The profanation of Sunday repeats the first sin over and over again. It is an attempt on *the* SANCTUARY *of the Lord!* Pain of death in both cases, and a terrible death at that... I spoke earlier about Eve's tears. The Fall is not a *fait accompli* of the past and something we submit to the consequences of. *We are always falling*, and now you know why *Eve weeps*. Her tears accompany us into the abyss.

Chapter 22: The Caterini Affair

There is no way to understand the enormous sacerdotal, and above all *episcopal*, prevarication, relative to the Miracle of La Salette, when one is unaware of the Caterini affair. Here is a quick summary then of that miserable story.

Mélanie's Secret begins with these words: **Mélanie, what I am about to tell you right now will not always be a secret: you can publish it in 1858.**[89]

In 1858, Mélanie was shut up in the Carmel of Darlington, in England. She asked to leave to complete her mission. When she returned, in 1860, the gravity of the Secret frightened members of the clergy when she spoke to them about it. She limited herself from then on to giving them a copy of her manuscript. It is in that way that numerous copies of it were distributed before 1870.

Many publications followed. The one that appeared in 1872 was honored with Pius IX's blessing. The one that appeared in 1873 was approved by the Cardinal Xyste-Riario Sforza, Archbishop of Naples. The one that appeared in 1879 was published by the Shepherdess herself, with the *imprimatur* by Mgr. de Lecce, the Count Zola, her director of conscience.

It is then when French priests, religious, and many bishops, wanting to make Rome condemn

---

[89] Original footnote: *1858!* The year of the Apparition of Lourdes!

Mélanie's brochure, that Mgr. Cortet, Bishop of Troyes, took it upon himself to sound the alarm.

Mgr. Cortet, not well informed on the rules of canonical Law in these matters, addressed himself to the Congregation of the Index, which redirected him to the Inquisition. Even there, he could not obtain anything. At the end of his wits, he approached the cardinal Caterini, a simple deacon but secretary by seniority of that Congregation of the Index, and he threatened him with *withdrawal of St. Peter's Denier* "if he did not do some thing (sic) about it." The secretary, 85 years old, signed the following letter drawn up by his sub-secretary:

> *Most Reverend Lord, Your letter dated July 23, relative to the publication of the opuscule entitled: –* The Apparition of the Holy Virgin on the Mountain of La Salette *– has been sent on to the Very Eminent Cardinals, Inquisitors of the Faith including me, who want you to know that the Holy See has seen with displeasure the publication that has been made and that its will is that copies already distributed should be, as much as possible,* withdrawn from the hands of the faithful...

> *– Rome, August 8, 1880. P. Cardinal Caterini.*

On receipt of that letter, Mgr. Cortet was floored, for it was not a condemnation. – First of all,

Rome does not say "withdrawn as much as possible" when it condemns a book. – Secondly, it was a private letter that one had sent him and nowise a decree, for it is obligatory that, in a decree, the Holy Office's date of reunion be given. – Thirdly, in lieu of the dotted line, which will be explained in a moment, there were these words: "*But let's keep it (*the brochure*) in the hands of the clergy, so that they might profit thereby.*" That last phrase was, in reality, an approbation of the brochure. Impossible to publish that.

Mgr. Cortet sent that response to his colleague in Nimes. Mgr. Besson didn't let so small a thing as that get in his way. He suppressed the last line, replaced it by a dotted line and published it, under guise of a decree, that private letter, truncated, falsified, and which was not even addressed to him. Mgr. de Troyes imitated him. A great number of *Semaines religieuses*[90] hastened to follow suit, even though they knew what it was. The *Revues catholiques*, the "good journals," were asked to insert it and did so in good faith, one hopes. Everyone believed, or wanted to believe, that Mélanie's brochure was *condemned*!

Later, the Missionaries of La Salette, estimating that the dotted line said too much even, replaced it with a single point, and slid their little paper by the thousands into the pilgrims' hands. At the same time, the calumnies made good progress; there was no doubt about it: "Mary's Child had perverted the message; she had gotten lost by vanity, unfaithful to her mission, etc."

Here, on that same subject, is a letter by

---

[90] *Semaines religieuses*: religious weeklies.

Mélanie to M. the Abbot Roubaud, curate of Vins, in the diocese of Fréjus, passed away in 1897, leaving behind a high reputation of holiness:

My very Reverend Father,

Do not trouble yourself with all that the demon does by means of men; the good God allows it in order to strengthen the faith of true believers... The individuals to whom I have addressed myself in Rome belong, the one to the Congregation of the Index and the other to that of the Holy Office or the Inquisition which is the same thing. Neither of them have any knowledge of Cardinal Caterini's letter. This is what was said to them, that there is a party who acts independently of the Pope and even of the Congregation of Indexes and of the Inquisition...

– Castellammare, October 25, 1880.

She wrote as well to Mgr. Pennachi, counselor of the Index, who gave her the same response. Mgr. Zola, Bishop of Lecce, who had given the *imprimatur*, went directly to Rome to obtain an explanation. The sub-secretary who had written the letter very humbly asked Mgr. de Lecce's pardon, telling him that his hand had been forced by the Bishop of Troyes and other bishops of France. The formulaic expressions that compromised, in this affair, "the

Most Eminent Cardinals" and "the Holy See" were plain *nonsense*!!![91]

Here, to conclude, is what Mélanie wrote, on October 13, 1880: "... The most guilty party with respect to the letter by cardinal Caterini is Mgr. Fava. However, there is nothing so opportune as the warnings by our compassionate Mother Mary, on the day before the religious are chased out... as the Secret, which one rejects, so well puts it... **Darkness obscures their intelligences**; are we not seeing those words of the Secret performed to the letter, before our very eyes!... A bishop wrote to the Congregation of the Index, and a Cardinal, secretary of the Congregation of the Inquisition, responds with a *private* and unofficial letter, and that *private* letter is reproduced in the religious weeklies, then subsequently in the religious journals, and thus makes its way around the world!!!... The Secret, inopportune for the faithful, excites everyone's curiosity and, from every quarter, I receive letters asking me for a copy of my little book which I no longer have. Look just how far the wisdom and prudence of opportunism have gone... To tell the truth, we are plunged in darkness! And it is a chastisement by God. *By stopping the diffusion of the Secret, one takes on a very great responsibility before God!* One will answer before God for the entire Message of the Virgin Mary! I would not wish to be in those people's shoes on the day of terrible

---

[91]Original footnote: The Cardinal Prosper Caterini, *secretary* and not *prefect* of the Congregation, as was published in error at the time, born in 1795, first deacon with the title of Holy Mary in *Via Lata*, died a year later, in October 1881, at the age of 86 years old. *Requiescat in pace*, as well as Mgr. Cortet, who died only several years ago.

Judgment!..."

Chapter 23: Mélanie's Sanctity. Apostles of the Last Days Prophesied by Her and by the Venerable Grignion de Montfort

To all that, Mélanie had only to oppose her sanctity, her immense beauty of a soul which was universally, I do not say misunderstood, but *unknown*. The least hostile people have the charity of hoping that she is not eternally lost, that she will end up by being admitted into Paradise, well below the ladies, after passing through Purgatory, the thought of which makes one shiver. The legends made up by the demon are so tenacious that, for a long time afterwards, one will believe that the Shepherdess of La Salette ended up badly; that after an extraordinary grace, which the least pious child of the small catechism would have been more worthy of, she relapsed, almost immediately, into lukewarm zeal, into indolence of the soul, into vanity, into infidelity, into deceit.[92] When one knows what to expect, that old mud from hell's mudscrapers

---

[92]Original footnote: In the following year, an arrogant ecclesiastic who had accused Mélanie of being a FORGER was himself brought to court for forging documents. *Sicut fecit sic fiet ei.*

seems so low and smells so bad that there is no way to stop it for one instant.

It was Mélanie's will that her directors of conscience or confessors should reveal nothing of her *private* life. But, from 1852 on, many people knew through Father Sibillat, who had obtained several confidences from that privileged child, whom, long before 1846, Heaven had visited her, that the great Apparition of 1846 was merely a single *episode* in her childhood; and the women Religious of Corenc, her companions, were able to observe that those graces did not stop. One has proof that they never stopped.

"That humble girl," – said her future historian whom it is not my place to name – "whom souls, even religious ones, cannot, before her private Life is published, suspect the lofty sanctity of and her great mission in the Church, – she was filled, since the age of three, with the most astonishing supernatural gifts, such as one finds in the lives of some saints. Instructed by the Baby Jesus who had taught her that she needed to hide her graces, she hid them with a great deal of humility and hability; and, when one discovered them, one saw just how much that discovery made her suffer, her directors themselves not knowing the half of it. In the mountains where she tended flocks before the Apparition, already she was called *the little saint,* and miracles were attributed to her."

Today it is known that she made miracles and the proof will be given when the Congregation of Rites deigns to take up the Beatification of so poor a Shepherdess. The discovery of stigmata has been a most fortuitous thing. She herself appeared *not to know* about them – even though she hid them, as with everything else, instinctively – or at least, she appeared to believe that *all Christians must have been like her* – which verges on a most terrifying sublimeness. Mélanie was often given communion by Our Lord himself and enjoyed the continual sight of her Guardian Angel. The inhabitants of Altamura have affirmed, having heard coming from the apartment of "the pious French woman," during the evening Angelus, on the night she passed away, angelic singing, and the ringing of a small bell, as when one carries the Holy Viaticum.

How many other things still! But what surprises most of all, what discourages thought, what gives an inestimable value to the single tears of love is this, that she is said to have seen *everything bathed in the Light of God*, not simultaneously, but successively, that is to say at the moment when her thought lit on an object. Extraordinary gift, unique perhaps in the life of the saints. She seemed to live in an earthly Paradise as if the Fall of man had never happened...

The following fragment regarding what Mélanie called her "Vision"[93] was communicated to a believer who wanted to know more about the Apostles of the Last Days:

"... In other places, I saw the Disciples of the Apostles of the Last Days. I understood quite clearly that those gentlemen, whom I call the Disciples, belonged to the Order. These were free men, young men who,

---

[93]Original footnote: This page, never published, completes or confirms what was said earlier, chap. XVI, of the gift of prophesy conferred on the Shepherdess.

not feeling themselves called to the sacerdocy, want-
ing however to embrace Christian life, accompanied
the Fathers on some missions, and worked with all
their energy for their own sanctification and the sal-
vation of souls. They were very zealous for the glory
of God. Those disciples were found beside the ill who
did not want to be confessed, beside the poor, the
wounded, prisoners, at public reunions, at sectarian
assemblies, etc., etc. I saw among them even those
who ate and drank with the impious, with those who
did not want to hear tell of God or priests; and you
could see how the terrestrial Angels tried by every
means imaginable to speak with them and to lead
them to God, and to save those poor souls, each one
of whom is worth the Blood of Jesus Christ, mad with
love for us. That vision was very clear, very precise,
and left no doubt in my mind as to what I saw; and I
admired the grandeur of God, his love for men, and
the holy industries he made use of to save everyone;
and I saw that his love cannot be understood on earth
because it exceeds anything that even the most holy
of men can conceive of...

"... Among them (the women Religious), there
were also women and girls filled with zeal who
helped the women religious in their work. Those wid-
ows and girls were people who, although not daring
to take religious vows, desired to serve the good God,
attend to their salvation, and lead a life withdrawn
from the world. They were dressed in black and very
simply. They wore also a cross on their chest, like the
Disciples, but a smaller one than the Missionaries
did, and it was not visible on the outside.

"... The Disciples and the women made also this promise or oblation to the Very Holy Virgin: to dedicate themselves to Her and to give to Her, for the souls in Purgatory, in favor of the conversion of sinners, all their prayers, all their penances, and, in a word, all their meritorious work.

"I saw that the Missionaries lived in community... I saw that the disciples who knew how to read said the Office in their chapel; I saw also that the women Religious recited the Office of the Holy Virgin as well as the lay women."

It is immensely interesting to compare that *vision*, so present, so precise, of the Shepherdess, with the less specific but so eloquent prophesy written 150 years before La Salette, by the Venerable Grignion de Montfort:

"... But what will the servants, slaves, and children of Mary be like? They will be a burning fire of ministers of the Lord who will spread the fire of divine love everywhere and, sicut sagittæ in manus potentis, *like sharp arrows in the hands of the powerful Mary to pierce her enemies with; they will be the children of Levi, well purified by the fire of great tribulations and adhering to God, who carry the gold of love in their heart, the incense of orison in their mind, and the myrrh of mortification in their body, and who will everywhere be the good odor of Jesus Christ for the poor and for the weak; as well they will be an odor of death for the great, for the rich, and for the proud, worldly folk.*

"They will be thunder clouds, flying through

*the air, on the least breath of the Holy Ghost, which,
without being attached to anything, nor being surprised by anything, nor being troubled by anything,
will pour the rain of God's word and of eternal life;
they will thunder against the sinner, they will grum-
ble against the world, they will strike the devil and
his henchmen, and they will pierce through and
through, for life or for death, with their double-edged
sword of God's word, all those to whom they will be
sent on the part of the Almighty.*

"They will be the veritable Apostles of the
Last Days *to whom the Lord of virtues will give the
word and strength to operate marvels and to bring
back glorious spoils from their enemies; they will
sleep without gold or silver, and, what is more, without trouble in the midst of other priests, ecclesiastics,
and clerics,* inter medios cleros, *and nevertheless
they will have the silvered wings of the dove, to go
where the Holy Ghost calls them*[94]*with the pure intention of the glory of God and the salvation of souls;
and they leave behind them, in the places where they
have preached, only the gold of the charity that is the
accomplishment of the law in its entirety. Finally, we
know that these will be the true disciples of Jesus
Christ, who, walking in the footsteps of his poverty,
humility, charity, and disdain for the world, will
teach the narrow path of God in pure truth, according to the holy Gospel, and not according to worldly
maxims, without concerning themselves with nor
causing acceptation of anyone, without sparing, listening to, or fearing any mortal, however powerful he*

---

[94]Original footnote: Ps. 67:14. Pentecost Matins. This mysterious
psalm belongs liturgically to the Holy Ghost.

might be.[95]

"They will have in their mouth the two-edged sword of God's word; they will carry on their shoulders the bloody banner of the Cross, the Crucifix in their right hand, the rosary in their left, the sacred Names of Jesus and Mary in their heart, and the modesty and mortification of Jesus Christ in all their bearing. Those will be the great men who come; but Mary will be there, by order of the Almighty, to extend his empire over that of the impious, idolaters, and Mohammedans. When and how will that be done?... God only knows; it is up to us to remain silent, to pray, to sigh, and to wait: Expectans, expectavi."[96]

Assuredly, God only knows. However we also know, we others, why and how that has not happened; why, on the upcoming September 19, 62nd anniversary of the Apparition, there will not be even a hint of the beginning of its execution, not a remote desire of obedience. We know only too well the sordid and base causes of that unheard-of prevarication. But not everyone knows, and it is for those, above all, who do not know, that this book was written. The others, the truly culpable by malice or by cowardice, will naturally try to stifle it, as best they can, simply by consistency of thought, without shame or fear. How to instill fear in men consecrated to God who could *see* the

---

[95]Original footnote: Almost literal conformity with the 30th paragraph of Mélanie's Secret, cited in the introduction of the present work.

[96]Original footnote: *Treatise of the True Devotion to the Holy Virgin*, 1st part, chapter 1.

terrible chastisement of so large a number clerical colleagues in their midsts without pounding their chest?... Finally, I have wanted to give testimony in order to be able to sleep in peace when my time comes.

La Salette's threats were conditional. There is room to believe that they are no longer. The Apostles of Mary, who should have been appointed before the Deluge of blood and fire, will come *later*, and that's all there is to it.

Chapter 24 Objections, Calumnies, the Assumptionist Drochon

My task is not done yet? I believe I have said all that needed to be said, and there is nothing more I can do now but repeat myself. A list of objections have been presented against the Secret which continue to hold currency at La Salette. I know them all too well, and I have refuted them implicitly or explicitly in the preceding pages. One knows, besides, that objections put forward by hatred, pride, or personal interest are invincible. They are reborn as soon as one strikes them down. But a distinctive trait of theirs is extreme flimsiness, an infantile flimsiness, to the effect that one is ashamed to hear them.

For example, "If the Pope wanted the Secret to be published, he would have done it himself." That objection, in the mouth of priests who pass for instructed, astonishes and afflicts. One feels that it would be quite pointless to tell them that the Pope was able to, and wanted to, *respect* Mélanie's mission, which was evident to him, and that he gave proof of that respect. Such an idea would not enter into such heads. So how to hope to make those slaves of the *letter* understand, those Helots of the vocable, that because the Pope is infallible, his SILENCE *is an approbation*? Now, the Secret has never been condemned. Let us add that this would be a question per-

haps of knowing whether it is according to the great
Rules that the Pope must personally see to such a document's publication?

And then, what to say in response to old
calumnies that habituation has transformed into indisputable truths, and that no Christian is advised to look
into the provenance of? At stake here is not just the
shame of the spirit, but the horror of the soul, and it is
abominable to think about the lies that have been refuted so many times, and so vainly confused!

An Assumptionist Father, named Drochon,
brought them all together in an *Illustrated History of
French Places of Pilgrimage*, a formidable work in
quarto, of 1274 pages (which would take 2548 men to
read, Barbey d'Aurevilly would have said), published
with the authorization and admiration of Father Picard, his general superior.[97] The Assumptionists are
known to have been the most constant enemies of
Mélanie and her Secret, and they were assiduous in
that war with all the force and authority that their extraordinary and lamentable success gave them in sup-
pressing publications.[98]

In that Father Drochon's enormous, massive

----

[97] Original footnote: Paris, Plon, 1890.

[98] Original footnote: One knows also that, for more than half a
century now, it is a sign of *modesty*, among modern Catholics, to
write in an appalling manner, and that that is painstakingly taught
in their Institutes, to the degree that all that was written after
Oraisons funèbres or *Henriade* is deemed negligible, unsettling,
or libidinous. The sublime Father Picard affirmed to me, one day,
to his order's shame, that Ernest Hello was a FOOL. His
successor, Father Bailly, and his Eliakims at the *Cross* or the
Pilgrim have really abused this doctrine.

work, *thirteen* pages only are given to the Shrine of La Salette, and it is almost impossible to find one line in it that is not inexact nor deceitful. One may judge for himself:

"... *Maximin and Mélanie would have received, as we have said, each their (sic) secret: 'infirm* and faltering if you will in everything else,' *said M. the Abbot Nortet, 'they are found to be strong in one single area only, which they have affirmed to be their mission.' 'Those children,' exclaimed in turn Mgr. Ginoulhiac, on September 19, 1855 (he had exiled Mélanie the year before),* '*can* go and be unfaithful to the great grace they received *(!), [but] the Apparition of Mary will not be shaken.' These citations foreshadow the vicissitudes that have left their mark on the life of the two children... Mélanie, after having contemplated the Queen of Heaven,* did not shut her eyes to the world *(!!!), as we have seen Anglèse de Saguzun, Liloye, and so many others do, as Bernadette did not long afterwards. She entered,* of course, *the convent of the Sisters of Providence of Corenc; but* believing herself *called to something important, dreaming of missions and apostolic conquests, sister Mary of the Cross inspired serious doubts about her vocation in religious life, which is* only effective if it is humble *(!!!). After her* three years *(one year) of novitiate, Mgr. Ginoulhiac op-*

posed her profession after being consulted.[99] *She re-*
turned to Corps where a Roman prelate of English
origin persuaded *her to follow him to England, with*
the design of having her dedicate herself to penance
for the conversion of her country. From 1854 to
1860, she stayed at the convent of the Carmelites of
Darlington. She wore the habit, took vows *it appears*
(!) in 1856, but *she returned to France four years lat-*
er to set herself up *in Marseille where,* according to
(!) M. Amédée Nicolas, her vows were retracted. She
stayed there until 1867. (No mention of Corfu, etc.)
Mgr. Louis Zola, Bishop of Lecce in Italy at that time,
led *her into his diocese and set her up at Castellam-*
mare (Admirable! Mgr. Zola was not yet a bishop at
this time; it's Mgr. Petagna who is involved here and
he did not lead *Mélanie* anywhere*; also, Castellam-*
mare is not in the diocese of Lecce, it is in another
bishopric altogether and it is quite far from Lecce. It

---

[99]Original footnote: Mgr. Ginoulhiac said to Mélanie: "I have just seen Maximin who has refused to tell me his secret, to me, his bishop!!! *He will repent it!!!* But you, you are more reasonable, you have more familiarity than him; I think that you are not going to refuse to obey your bishop...!!!" And on the refusal by that poor child to disobey the Holy Virgin, he made the same threat: "*You will repent it!*" He kept his word only too well. When the moment came for her to make her profession, to pronounce her vows among the Sisters of Providence of Corenc, he opposed it, despite the Sisters saying how pious she was, and he sought, by all possible means and vexations, to make her depart. Finally, he had her sent off to England, forbidding her to tell her parents even. Even better, he gave orders to have her forced to make a vow of cloister. When she refused to do it, because of the mission she would have to fulfill after 1858, and that no pressure, no insistence, could vanquish her resistance, the sisters told her: "Where will you go? Mgr. G*** has written to us that you will return to his diocese, he will excommunicate you everywhere you reside."

is as if one were to situate Amiens in the diocese of Périgueux. The Assumptionists are not very strong in geography. The historian got his information from a good source, someone or other of the Missionaries of La Salette, and his book is thick). On the death of the bishop, in 1888, (neither Mgr. Petagna nor Mgr. Zola were dead in 1888), she came back to Marseille where she is still (1890). In the midst of that tumultuous and inconstant *life, Mélanie has remained virtuous (Ah! you don't say! just barely virtuous!) and, like Maximin, persevering* on a single article, *her ardent faith (After what has preceded, the word* ardent *is all the more stupid, but that's how it is when one writes as an Assumptionist) in the Apparition and in the Secret that she had heard." (And not a single word about that secret! It is as if Mélanie's publication and Mgr. Zola's* imprimatur *were apocryphal, given that, on the other hand, Drochon says that the Secret is the "key" to the Apparition – in the style of Bailly, in the style of the* Cross *and the* Pilgrim.)

That page brings to my mind something that Châteaubriand said: "These days one must be economical with one's disdain, because there is a large number of people who are in need of it."

Chapter 25: The Hostelry. The Missionaries or Chaplains' Double Tactic

Since I first began this work, pious people of pure intention thought my reproach of the hostelry of La Salette was excessive.[100] Pilgrims must be given room and board, they told me, and principally the infirm and ill, but they cannot expect to be lodged and fed for nothing. Now, that is precisely what they should expect. The strict right of pilgrims, principally the infirm and ill, is to be given room and board *for nothing.* In October 1880, at the time of the so-called missionaries, I saw a beggar arrive one morning at the hostelry door, during a terrible snow; he was scarcely less white than the snow, and he appeared to be about eighty years old. He said he had walked up the mountain for hours, certain to find at La Salette the two days of hospitality that vagabonds by a rule of hostelry are assured to find. I have never seen that rule, dreamt up perhaps by poor wretches, but what I did see, and see all too well, is the despair, the humble despair of that old man, telling me, a quarter of an hour later: "They gave me a bowl of cold soup and told me I had to leave. I really could have used some

---

[100]Original footnote: I expressed myself much more strongly still, at the time of the Missionaries. *The Woman Who Was Poor*, pages 100 and 101.

rest." So as not to be complicit in a murder, and although very poor myself, I paid three days of pension
for that visitor, who maybe was the angel Raphael,
and whose gratitude stayed with me like a soft light in
a condemned man's cell.

From that day forward, I understood what was
happening on that mountain. To speak frankly, I saw
the dreadful spirit of avarice of those so-called religious who shouldn't have been anything but beggars
themselves and the servants of beggars, for La Salette
is, by essence and *par excellence*, a place of pilgrimage for barefoot vagabonds. Let them come to the
foot of that mountain all they want, and often as they
want, but once arrived they cannot climb up it *deli-
cately* without the devil on their back. The first pilgrims were not deceived and could not have been deceived. The current route didn't exist back then, and
the mule service did not operate like it does today.
One saw them, the infirm, the dying, the half-dead,
dragging themselves up the sides of the Mountain,
those who took entire days to crawl up and who came
back down it healed. Mlle. des Brulais, who was one
of the first witnesses of La Salette, has related several
really prodigious examples.[101] I don't believe it would
be possible to cite a single case of any of those ill
people on the Mountain dying. But how hard it is for
human beings to pass the night without a roof over
their head, without a tent, *sub Jove frigido*, at that
mortal altitude and deprived of shelter! What help
could the shelter of several cabins be, made of plank

---

[101]Original footnote: *The Holy Mountain's Echo*, by Mlle. DES
BRULAIS. Henri Douchet publisher, Méricourt-l'Abbé (Somme).
There is no better book on the beginnings of La Salette.

boards, for the hundreds and thousands of pilgrims? *Quid inter tantos*? But they came spurred on by faith; they were attended to, warmed, recomforted, healed by faith.

Today, one climbs up comfortably in a car or on the back of a mule; one pays for his room and board, 1st or 2nd class; one prays at his ease, with the shelter of real walls, in a well-sealed basilica, and one is surprised not to obtain what one seeks. One is not a Pharisee perhaps, but one does not believe himself to be, *sicut ceteri hominum*, a robber, an unjust person, an adulterer; and one has no fear "lifting his eyes to heaven." Then one goes back down the mountain in the same car or on the back of the same mule, but not like the poor publican. *Descendit hic justificatus (*hoc est *sanatus) in domum suam.*[102] There are no more miracles because there are no more believers nor PENITENTS, because there is no more enthusiasm, that is to say charity. **There are no more generous souls**.

One would gasp to find a sales counter or accounting books in the antechamber of a poet, but one is not at all surprised to see those same objects in a place of pilgrimage, and what a place of pilgrimage! It is stupefying to tell oneself that there is a place where the Holy Virgin has appeared, where she wept with love and compassion, where she said the greatest things that one has ever heard since Isaiah, where she healed and consoled so many miserable souls, and where two paces away from that place is a *cash register*!

---

[102]*Descendit... suam*: Latin for "He went back down from there justified (that is *healed*) to his own home."

"It is abominable," you say, "but what to do about it?" You know as well as I do. Transformed into a House of God, where each able-bodied pilgrim would act as a servant or a nurse to the poor, for several hours or several days – the hostelry of La Salette would be superabundantly and constantly provisioned, if Christians gave it the hundredth part of what they so pointlessly and with so much bitterness give to the tax collector. It would be twenty times richer than now, too rich doubtless, but at least one would no longer hear the tinkling sound of money that God detests, and one would have the joy and the glory of re-animating countless poor people.

That there honestly, in a nutshell, is what the shepherds could have understood, and it is not without fright that I imagine what must have passed through Maximin's gentle and noble heart when he was a witness to the exploitation on his Mountain, when he was dying of misery several paces away from the sordid religious who owed their existence to him. As for old Mélanie, what things she must have felt when she made the pilgrimage, one last time, before her death, – I have already asked myself, and all I can come up with is tears.

I have said it enough already, – my book has but one object: to prove that all the effort expended by God's enemies, in the case of La Salette, has been aimed at discrediting Mélanie's Secret, which is the only one in question, given that Maximin's has never been divulged. So, double tactic. On the one hand, the Missionaries or Chaplains who were installed on the Mountain have always and very firmly wanted the

Holy Virgin's threats to be fulfilled, not long after the Apparition, in an entirely complete and definitive way, such that it would be demonstrated that we have no longer anything to fear and that all other prophesy about the future or even the present would have to be taken for nonsense. I have seen them working, every day, near the Fountain, at the hour of Recitation, pointing to the statistics of famine in Ireland, brought on by the potato blight; in France, in Spain, or in Poland, by the blight of wheat, etc. As for the menace in the Discourse relative to the "little children under the age of seven...", it appears that that is very sufficiently explained by a deplorable epidemic that took place around the same time, that is to say, sixty years ago. Consequently, the so-called Secret is nothing more than a very apocryphal, malicious revery that good Catholics ought to sweep away.

Then again, one needs to consider the difference of time. In 1846, Religion was despised and Christian society had need of being chastised. Today it is, on the contrary, in a most flourishing state, doesn't anyone see it? In any case, the Secret is untenable.

On the other hand, one really wishes that the Shepherds hadn't persevered *on one point*: Maximin, a drunk according to the ignoble and criminally false legend propagated by the Missionaries, never leaving his drunken stupor except to tell, by constant miracle, the story of the Apparition with *lucidity*; Mélanie, a holy girl, if you will, but given to the most dangerous vagabondage and continually "surrounded by cranks and disobedient priests who went to her head," not finding again, just like Maximin, her equilibrium and her reason except when it was a question of retelling the story of that same Apparition, identically related by her since 1846. Outside the cut-and-dry public Discourse, which it is impossible to cast doubt on without condemning it to non-existence, how can one suppose a secret of life and death divulged supererogatorily by such witnesses?

After that, the interested parties could say, if one wished to go to the trouble of considering these things coldly, reasonably, *practically*, – how not to see, O Mother of the Verb, that your so-called Revelation is nothing more than an imposture put forward by demons to prevent religious saints from honestly gaining their livelihood on your Mountain?

Chapter 26: La Salette and Louis XVII

Excellent historical works have recently elucidated the question of the survival of Louis XVII. An already old matter that one can no longer ignore today without a bit of shame. My *Fils de Louis XVI*, published in 1900, did not put forward any new documentary evidence, but rather the testimony of an infinite admiration for that great gesture of God, unique in History: A royal Race that passed for the first in the world, not exactly rejected, nor exterminated, but fallen into unsoundable ignominy, with no hope ever of rising out of it.

"... It's enough to make one's head spin to tell oneself that there once was a man without bread, without a roof over his head, without family, without a name, without a country, an individual like any other lost in the crowds, whom the lowest of churls could insult and who was, however, the King of France!... The King of France recognized as such, in secret, by all the governments whose titulars sweated with anguish at the very thought that he might still be alive, that one could run into him at any moment, and that he couldn't give a fig whether poor France, completely stricken as it was, seeing his sorrowful face pass by in street, did not immediately recognize in him the Blood of its ancient Masters and did not rush towards him with a loud cry, in a sublime moment of enthusiasm for his resurrection!

"One did what one could to kill him. The most barbaric imprisonments, knife, fire, poison, calumny, fierce ridicule, dark misery and black chagrin, all were employed. One succeeded in the end, when God had had enough of watching over him and when he was sixty years old already, that is to say when he had succeeded in bearing his penance of sixty kings..."[103]

The disgrace of that "phantom King's" was so perfect that the words "ignominy" or "opprobrium" no longer suffice. He was refused something that the worst villains are not refused, a personal identity, – to say it better, any identity whatsoever. One absolutely wanted in no uncertain terms that he should be nobody, in the strictest acceptation of the word, and that his children should be nobody's children. Thus was fulfilled, in a way that God alone could invent, the secular Capetian formula: *The King does not die*, because Louis XVI's legitimate descendance was condemned no longer to live or die.

The Dauphin, Louis XVI's son, – the authentic Louis XVII, – presumed dead at the Temple, in 1795, took his last breath at Delft, in Holland, on August 10, 1845, a little more than thirteen months before the Apparition of La Salette, "particularly exact promptitude of that miracle, so short a while after the Candelabra with the Golden Lilies, mentioned in the Pentateuch, had been knocked over.

---

[103]Original footnote: LÉON BLOY. *The Son of Louis XVI*. This is not the place to show, even if foreshortened, the frightening and phantasmagoric history of Louie XVII. One should read *The Last Legitimate King of France*, by HENRI PROVINS, and the more recent, inestimable work by OTTO FRIEDRICHS: *Louis XVII's Intimate and Unpublished Correspondence*.

"When news of the Apparition had come out, a single Christian asked himself if something infinitely precious was not about to be broken, such that Splendor itself, impassible and inaccessible Glory, should appear in mourning? – **For all the time that I've suffered for you others!** What a troubling and inconceivable phrase!

"The catastrophe is so enormous that that which absolutely cannot suffer suffers nevertheless and weeps. Beatitude sobs and begs. The Almighty declares that it cannot go on like this and asks for mercy... What happened then, if not that Someone died who ought not to have died?..."[104]

Again, if he had really died as everyone else dies, but, I repeat, it was much worse, the King of France is not supposed to die. And here it is more than sixty years later and that continues! I have here before me the portrait of a poor little child of 4 or 5 years old, whom one calls the Prince Henri-Charles-Louis de Bourbon, Dauphin de France. It appears that it is he who will continue the line of phantom Kings....

Many letters by Mélanie, some of which to the Princesse Amélie de Bourbon, prove that the prophetess had no doubt about the Survival represented by the pretender Naundorff[105] and his children. In 1881, she names his direct heir as the "*legitimate King,*

---

[104]Original footnote: *The Son of Louis XVI.*

[105]Naundroff: Karl Wilhelm Naundorff (1785-1845), a German clockmaker, who, among others, claimed to be Louis XVII of France.

King FLEUR DE LYS," and recommends hope. One knows besides that, many years before, Maximin had taken a trip to Frohsdorf and that a meeting there with the Count de Chambord had had for a result the effective renunciation by this latter person to the throne of France. All which leads one to believe that, in effect, Maximin would have said to that pretender what Martin de Gallardon, in 1816, had said to the infamous Louis XVIII: "You are an usurper." The Count de Chambord, contrary to his fratricidal great uncle, did not dare succeed the two Cains of the Restoration, but all the same he kept the 300 million francs of royal patrimony, and the robbed heirs, for three generations, continued to be poor and covered with the most abundant ignominy, as their father had been, and principally their grandfather, the Dauphin du Temple.

Analogy or affinity, correspondence or mysterious relation, between the Miracle of La Salette and the miracle of the fate of the Son of Louis XVI. A poor king, a king dying of hunger and poverty, the son covered in filth and obstinately repudiated by sixty kings, comes out and offers to save France, and one murders him after his having been flagellated for so long a time. *Nolumus hunc regnare super nos.*[106]

Soon afterwards, the real Queen of France, the Sovereign to whom the Kingdom was authentically, validly and irrevocably given, she in turn comes forward in tears, supplicating her people and all other peoples of whom that kingdom is the Oldest son, to look at the frightening Gulf that *invokes* them... Unable to kill her, they respond to her with Disobedi-

---

[106]*Nolumus... nos*: Latin for "We refuse to let him rule over us."

ence, Negation of her words, and the Judaic lapidation of her witnesses. *Nolumus HANC regnare super nos.*

I have thought, many times, that God's patience is the best proof of Christianity.

Today, is it all a lost cause? Is there nothing left to hope for? Are there no other remedies than chastisement? The author of this book is convinced of it. France no longer wants a King, nor a Queen, nor God, nor the Eucharist, nor Penance, nor Pardon, nor Peace, nor War, nor Glory, nor Beauty, nor whatever it might be that gives life or death. It wants, in its capacity as a mistress and as an example for other nations, what has never been wanted by any decadence: perfect stupidity in an artificial and automatic impulsion. That is called Sport, which has got to be one of the English words for Damnation.

In the year 1864, the Secret says, **Lucifer and a large number of Demons will have left Hell...**

One knows that Leo XIII, struck by that prediction, wanted all Catholic priests to recite, every day, after mass, kneeling at the foot of the altar, this prayer which is so similar to an exorcism:

SANCTE MICHAEL, ARCHANGELE, DEFENDE NOS IN PRÆLIO; CONTRA NEQUITIAM ET INSIDIAS DIABOLI ESTO PRÆSIDIUM. IMPERET ILLI DEUS, SUPLICES DEPRECAMUR; TUQUE, PRINCEPS MILITÆ CŒLESTIS, SATANAM ALIOSQUE SPIRTUS MALIGNOS QUI AD PERDITIONEM ANIMARUM PERVAGANTUR IN MUNDO, DIVINA VIRTUTE IN INFERNUM DETRUDE. AMEN.

Appendices

Appendix 1: Documentary Evidence

The document that follows, written in Mélanie's hand, will make known the source of calumnies repeated without end, for thirty years, against the Secret, the Rule of the Holy Virgin, the Seer, and her Mission.

... (Cusset, Allier), this February 28, 1904.[107] To Monsieur the Abbot H. Rigaux, curate of Argœves, near Dreuil-les-Amiens (Somme).

My very Reverend and very dear Father,

May Jesus be loved by all!

I had promised you, God willing, to put into writing my trip to Rome, what preceded it, the Congress held in Saint Peter's name by his Eminence the Cardinal Ferrieri, Prefect of the Congregation of Bishops and Regular Clergy, what was discussed there, my private audience with the Holy Father and what we spoke about, my entrance into the Salésiane order (the Visitandines), then my departure and what followed.

Until present, I have been unable to set that down on paper, because of an illness. May God be blessed for everything!

---

[107]Original footnote: Mélanie died on December 14 of the same year. This precious letter may be considered then as a sort of testament. It goes without saying that the Shepherdess' *style* has been scrupulously respected.

I

In the year of grace 1878 and, I believe, in October, one morning, after Holy Mass, the Reverend Father Fusco told me that he had read in a newspaper the intention of Mgr. Fava, Bishop of Grenoble, to come to Rome to obtain an approval for *his* Rule for the Fathers and Sisters of the Mountain of La Salette.

On hearing that news, I said: "In order to have a clear conscience, I will make haste to write down the Rule of the Very Holy Mother of God and send it to the Holy Father." "I will carry it myself to Rome," said Father Fusco. And everything proceeded according to plan.

About one month later, on a Sunday, my holy Bishop, Mgr. Pétagna, let me know that he wished to speak with me. On climbing the stairs, I met some good old canons who were shedding tears and saying: "It would have been better if he had stayed in his diocese and not come here to kill our Bishop. If it weren't for his soutane, I would take him for a haughty, imperious gendarme." Other canons told me: "Goodness gracious, put an end to the Bishop of Grenoble's cruel entreaties to Mgr. Pétagna, already rather ill." I asked them why the Bishop of Grenoble had given *orders* to my holy Bishop. I was told, "The Bishop of Grenoble, with an attitude of powerful authority, *orders* our holy Bishop to oblige you, to constrain you, to go into his Diocese, etc., etc." – I enter, and, for the first time, I see Mgr. Fava.

The Bishop of Grenoble was accompanied by a priest whom I discoverd later to be Father Berthier, one of the missionaries of La Salette.

Mgr. de Grenoble said to me, among other banal and indifferent things, that he had heard it said that I was here, and that he had come from very far away to see me. I thanked him. My holy Bishop, already ill, felt exhausted and had need of rest, and of calmness of mind principally. A domestic came in to tell him that his room was prepared, if he needed to rest. Then my holy Bishop said to me, "Mgr. de Grenoble and the R. Father Berthier will take their meal with you because here, since I have been suffering so much, one does not prepare anything, one no longer puts food on the table." While expressing to my holy Bishop my regret for his state of unwellness, I thanked him for the honor he gave me to provide for Monseigneur and his worthy Priest; then I entreated him to allow me to retire, so that I could prepare in advance of their visit. My holy Bishop, noticing Mgr. Fava's silence with respect to what we had just discussed, thought that he had not understood. He repeated it to him a second time, then a third time, and I went back home in order to prepare everything for the meal at noon.

At noon, Mgr. of Grenoble arrives with Father Berthier. The first words out of his mouth were: "I have come to Rome for three reasons: to have my rule for the Fathers and Sisters approved; to obtain the title of Basilica for the Church on the mountain of La Salette; and to have a NEW STATUE of Our Lady made, similar to the model I brought; because, you see, no statue represents well the Holy Virgin, who must not have a headscarf or an apron; and everyone murmurs and disapproves of that costume of women of the countryside. The model I have commissioned is much better! To start with, she will not wear a cross... for, you see, that makes pilgrims sad, and the Holy Virgin must not have a cross..."[108] I will skip what followed, my quill refuses to make known in detail all what his Greatness said. I was frightened; I nearly said to him: "And, at the base of your statue, Monseigneur, you will inscribe in large letters: '**Virgin of the Mgr. Fava's vision!**'" The meal was ready.

After the meal, the Bishop of Grenoble opened the doors to a balcony to look out at the landscape and above all Vesuvius which was in front of us. His Greatness asked me who we had for neighbors. I told him that we were alone.

"Oh! but you are lodged like a prince!" And he began to walk through the rooms. He exited the terrace that, when it was not raining, served as a place of recreation for my pupils. He contemplated Vesuvius for a long time again, the sea, the landscape... After which he came back, not without having opened and gone through my office; and, on seeing so many, many letters on my desk, he said to me: "But your correspondence is much greater than mine! Where did you get so many letters?" "From all over Europe, Monseigneur." "You are lodged in too fine a palace! It's so spacious here: you can take a walk without exiting..."

After about three quarters of an hour, or one hour, Monseigneur said that he was going to bid Mgr.

---

[108]Original footnote: I do not underline these last lines, Mélanie did not underline them either. One is asked only to notice them.

Pétagna goodbye, then take the train for Rome: "Oh! she will be ravishingly beautiful my statue: all in marble, with a fine coat that covers her; no shoes, no crucifix, – that saddens people too much; the Holy Virgin could not have been accoutered as you said." "Eh! well, Monseigneur," I said to him, "if the good God sent me his Providence, I would have a painting made where the Very Holy Virgin, Mother of God, was represented in between two resplendent lights, and adorned such as she appeared to me on the Mountain of La Salette." And Mgr. Fava left together with F. Berthier.

In the late afternoon, to my great surprise, a female messenger sent by my holy Bishop came to tell me that my holy Bishop had something to communicate to me.

I asked that person if Mgr. of Grenoble had departed. "Fortunately, he was on his way out," she responded, "when a messenger opened the door and gave to Mgr. Pétagna a letter from Rome to be communicated to you. Then, that Carbonaro Bishop came back, and he absolutely had to know the contents of that dispatch. He gave our Monseigneur a great deal of trouble." I departed with the same person for the Bishop's palace.

Arrived at the gate, I said to her, "Clearly Mgr. the Bishop of Grenoble will have remained; enter, and tell our Mgr. Pétagna that the person is waiting for him." Thus was it done.

My holy Bishop came out to me with the dispatch, and in a soft voice he told me more or less this:

"The Holy Father wishes to speak with you. Here is the dispatch insofar as it concerns you:

> *If Mélanie is not ill and if she can come to Rome, His Holiness would like to speak with her. If she cannot come, then she should send all that concerns the foundation of the new religious Order of the Apostles of the Last Days."*

I asked Monseigneur when I should depart.

"Today is Sunday," he said, "and rather too soon because of all the preparations you'll need to make. There's no hurry."

At that moment, the Bishop of Grenoble appeared and said: "Monseigneur, I believe that you have given Mélanie the *entirety* of her dispatch, you can now give it *to me*."

And my holy Bishop responded humbly, "Excuse me, Monseigneur, there are, in the dispatch, things for her and things for me. What I can tell you though is that she is summoned to Rome."

"Ah well! And do you know why? what business does she have there, Monseigneur?"

Silence on the part of my holy Bishop.

"Very well, we will depart this evening."

Then I said, "I do not travel on Sunday."

Mgr. of Grenoble: "But you must obey the Pope!"

"The Holy Father did not tell me to leave immediately on receipt of the dispatch."

Looking at my holy Bishop, Mgr. Fava said to him, "You must make her depart this evening with me, Monseigneur."

"Monseigneur, she cannot depart just like that. You must, if she has something to prepare, give her more time than that."

"Obey! obey! You know that I am the Bishop of Grenoble! and I have so many things to teach you, to say to you, and to ask of you. You see, it is this evening, at ten o'clock, that we must take the train for Rome. You will be there, won't you?"

"I do not know, Monseigneur."

"Ah! but you must!... Monseigneur," he exclaimed, "oblige her, command her to depart this evening with me."

My holy Bishop, pale as death, responded to him, "I do not possess the art of ordering people to obey commands at the drop of a feather. Any more than the Holy Father, I cannot know whether she has things to attend to before her departure."

To put an end to this conversation, I said that I was going to retire. That it was night.

The Bishop of Grenoble, after saying to me, "*Au revoir*, at ten o'clock!" returned to his room, and I was free to speak with and take orders from my holy Bishop, who said to me, "Monseigneur of Grenoble will be the death of me. If you can, leave this evening to get him off my back. I will give you Father Fusco and your companion. You will leave when you can, this evening, and may the good GOD bless you."

Back at home, we made our arrangements, thinking that I would stay in Rome for no more than two or three days. As I had sent the Rule of our Mother of God nearly a month earlier: "I believe," said Father Fusco, "that you are being sent for to hear something on the subject of the foundation of the Apostles of the Last Days. For the Bishop of Grenoble told us at the bishop's palace, that after having gone to the Sacred Congregation of Bishops and Regular Clergy in order to hasten the approval of his Rule, the Cardinal Ferrieri had made him understand that at that moment he was very busy and that Mgr. could, for at least one week, pass his time visiting the monuments of Rome and surrounding areas. That is why the Bishop of Grenoble came here."

We planned then to take the train at nine o'-clock in the evening from Castellammare.

At ten o'clock, we were in Naples. We had to wait for the train that was leaving for Rome. With GOD's leave!... the Bishop of Grenoble arrives all out of breath:

"I have been looking for you for half an hour!... Eh, well, come, we are going to take our seats."

I thanked the Monseigneur; I said that *we* always traveled in third class.

"But," he said, "is there someone else with

you?"

"A priest and my companion, Monseigneur."

"They can find seats in another wagon," the Monseigneur said. "Give me your ticket, I will have it upgraded it to first class."

I told him that my holy Bishop having had the goodness of giving me the company of those two individuals, I could not separate from them.

Nearly losing his temper, Monseigneur said: "I will upgrade their's as well. But do you know why you are summoned to Rome?"

I responded, "No, and I am not concerned about it."

We depart. The Bishop of Grenoble, who had so many things to say to me before, spoke not a word. But I was pained to see that Father Fusco and my companion were looked askance at and one might even say with anger.

Father Berthier had a dissatisfied look on his face: he had not succeeded, by closing the door, to keep my companions from climbing into our compartment; immediately the door opened, and Father Fusco, on entering, said:

"Excuse me, Monseigneur, if I take the liberty of entering here; it is to be in conformance with the wishes of our Mgr. the Bishop of Castellammare, who does not want me to leave Sister Mary of the Cross's side."

And the Bishop of Grenoble said nothing in response.

Monday, at seven o'clock in the morning, we arrived in Rome, and there, we separated. Monseigneur and Father Berthier went to the French Seminary, it seems to me; and we were in a Church where Father Fusco celebrated the Holy Mass. Afterwards, we were lodged at a hotel, where we stayed, I think, for more than a week.

On the very first day, I had my arrival announced to Cardinal Ferrieri to put myself at his disposition. His Eminence communicated to me that he would alert me in advance of the day he would have need of me.

We were at liberty then, every day after Holy Mass; and we spent the afternoons agreeably in God, by visiting the beautiful Churches of Santa Maria Maggiore, S. Paulo Fuori Le Mura, the Church that has a huge painting representing Our Lady of La Salette, and the Catacombs. But our first visits were to individuals known by us to be very believing, very devoted to Our Lady of La Salette, for example, the cardinals Consolini and Guidi, who graciously offered me their services under any circumstances. And I gave them both a copy of the Secret that I wanted to publish with the Imprimatur by Mgr. Pétagna, my holy Bishop of Castellammare di Stabia.

The Bishop of Grenoble, with great kindness, sent Father Berthier to check in on us every day, often two times a day; and that latter person above all questioned the Maître d' if we were often absent, if our absences were extended, if he knew where we went, what we did, and if we received any visitors. One day, I believe, the third, the maître d' told us:

"The priest who comes each day and who is with the Bishop of Grenoble came to tell me on the part of the Bishop that he was going to take it upon himself to pay all the expenses you incur here, and for the whole time you stay in Rome."

So as not to return to this later, I mention here that when I had to take up quarters with the Salésianes, and my companions had to return to Castellammare, I asked the maître d' to be so kind as to settle up with the Bishop of Grenoble. The Bishop responded that he did not recognize the bill.[109] The maître d' reminded him of the promise he had twice made. The Bishop said he wouldn't hear of it. That poor maître d' could not get over it. I took the bill then and I paid it, while consoling that poor gentleman.

I must also say here what I later learnt from a reliable source. Mgr. of Grenoble lost no time upon our arrival in Rome. He visited the Sacred Congregations, the Cardinals, the Bishops, to discover for what purpose, for what reason, the Shepherdess of La Salette "has been summoned to Rome." And if he got no satisfaction, he went elsewhere to inform himself. Someone said that the Cardinal Ferrieri had the Rule that the Holy Virgin had given to Mélanie, and that "the Secretary of Cardinal Ferrieri, Mgr. Bianchi, ought to be well apprised of those things." When the

---

[109]Original footnote: that passage, no more than the previous one, was not underlined by Mélanie.

Bishop of Grenoble had learnt that, he sought out Mgr. Bianchi, who announced to him that there was a Congress for that affair. The Bishop of Grenoble recognized in Mgr. Bianchi a man capable of helping him in his fight against "the Rule of Mélanie." The Bishop of Grenoble sought (or bought, I'm told) other prelates.

II

Towards the end of the week, the Cardinal Ferrieri has conveyed to me the day and hour that I was expected. We arrived ten minutes early. We remained in the waiting room during this time. At each instant someone rang: it was always bishops, and the person in charge of getting the door said to them:

"His Eminence is not receiving anyone: there is an extraordinary Congress..."

It was then, for the first time, that I knew I had come to a Congress. There were two or three Bishops, one after the other, who insisted on entering, and one of them said that he had been invited by the Bishop of Grenoble. They were not allowed to enter.

The hour passed, the Bishop of Grenoble did not come. The Cardinal Ferrieri had me brought in and seated next to him; while his secretary, Mgr. Bianchi, leafed through some papers.

The Cardinal said to me:

"How long has it been since you were on the mountain of La Salette?"

"I went in 1871."

"Are you familiar with them, those religious and their manner of life?"

"I do not know them in person: they have never spoken to me; not even to learn about the holy Apparition. As for their manner of living, private or public, I am told that they are but mediocre secular clergy, faithless, lacking in zeal, busying themselves only with amassing money, jealous, calumniators with hard hearts. That humbles me, Your Eminence, because it would be much worse than that for me, what I would do or what I might be, without God's grace."

"Have you seen anything? Have you been a witness to something that was not right according to God?"

"I will tell you, Your Eminence, what has struck me, what has left a deep impression on me. It was in 1851, I believe. While the Bishop of Grenoble sought every means possible to get rid of me by exile, he sent me to the mountain of La Salette for about one month. It was February. Despite the snow and the poor conditions along the path, every day some pilgrims arrived on mule back. One day a rich lady arrived. Then all the Fathers went out to meet her with great ceremony; and as the muleteer wanted to come inside as well, because he was the carrier of that lady's luggage and also because he needed some rest and something to eat, one Father took the luggage from him and closed the door sharply on that poor muleteer's face, who was chilled to the bone. He came to hear Mass on his knees. Towards the end of the Holy Sacrifice, that man fell over, making a great noise. I went to him to offer my assistance and have him sit down. Now, neither the Fathers, nor the people attached to their service, lifted a finger; nor, after mass, did anyone offer him anything to drink. Ah! if I have ever regretted being too poor, it was that day then, I hadn't even a centime! I went back and encountered Mme. Denaz, who said to me:

"'Go to the kitchen area, you will find your coffee.'

"I ran to the kitchen, took my cup, and quickly brought it to that poor man. After thanking me, he said:

"'You have restored me. When I left Corps, it was before sunrise. And then, walking in the snow for three hours, it was tiring. That Lady had made a request to have something to drink brought to me by the Fathers and at her expense; they did not let me in; and you will see whether they are well paid for what I did not have. It is always like that with these Fathers; also, they are not well liked.'

"I brought my cup back and Mme. Denaz (she was one of the sisters-in-law of the Fathers) said to me:

"'I am sure that you have not taken your breakfast, that you gave it to the muleteer. If you stay here for a long time, the house will quickly be without resources, and we will be lacking in everything.'

"Several days later, among the pilgrims who arrived, a poor man was discovered who was asking for alms from the strangers. By chance, I was in the Fathers' store when the poor mendicant, before leaving the Holy Mountain, wanted to buy a simple medal of Our Lady of La Salette. The person who was operating the store put the medal on the counter: the poor man takes it and kisses it with love, and the person takes the sou, but realizes it is only a half sou! Quickly, quickly, she calls the poor man back, throws the half sou at him, and takes back the medal (the half sou were still in circulation at that time in France).

"The poor man explained that all he had was the half sou, but it did not matter, the person was inflexible. Long story short, I gave a sou that I had and took the medal which I gave to that man. Up on the mountain, one does not know this, – when one gives to the poor, one gives to GOD.

"I took that opportunity while I was in the Fathers' store to assure myself that absolutely nothing but objects of piety were sold, as they had promised me. I found ornamental jewelry for the ladies, snuffboxes for the men, etc., etc.

"It seems to me, Your Eminence, that on that holy ground where the Very Holy Virgin had shed so many tears, where she reminded us of the observance of the sanctification of Sunday, it seems to me," I said, "that if those Fathers were penetrated with the loftiness of their mission, they would sacrifice their greed, they would be the first ones to set a good example, by closing their merchandise shops on the holy day of rest."

Then Mgr. of Grenoble comes into the room:

he salutes in military style, with his hand to his fore-
head. There is a small discussion at the door: it's Father Berthier who wants to enter too. The door is
closed, and we all sit down. The Congress begins.

The cardinal Ferrieri says this:

"Eh, well! Monseigneur, I am told that you
have made a Rule for your missionaries."

"Yes, Your Eminence."

"And did you know that the Holy Virgin had
given one to Mélanie?"

"Yes, Your Eminence, but my Rule is quite
different from Mélanie's."

"And how did you get it into your head to
make a Rule, when you knew that the Very Holy Virgin had given one to Mélanie?"

(Mgr. Fava remains SILENT.)

"But, at the very least, you consulted with
Mélanie in order to make your Rule?"

(Mgr. Fava remains SILENT.)

The cardinal, addressing himself to me, says:

"Did Monseigneur not consult with you when
he made his Rule?"

"No, Your Eminence, never."

"Eh, well! We order Mélanie to go onto the
Mountain of La Salette, with the Rule that she received from the Holy Virgin, and make the Fathers

and the women Religious observe it."

"Your Eminence," said Mgr. Fava, "I will not accept Mélanie's Rule until the Church **proves** to me that it comes from the Holy Virgin."

And Mgr. Bianchi, the secretary, who, according to ecclesiastical laws and Rules, was there only to transcribe what was asked, objections, responses, but **having been bought**, said:

"Your Eminence, you do not know that the women Religious are like this with Mélanie?"

And on saying those words he put his two index fingers together and tapped them.

Then I said:

"I have never spoken with the Sisters there. How could we be in disagreement. I'm not aware of it."

His Eminence asked me what I thought about what the Monseigneur of Grenoble had just said.

"I submit to all decisions of the Holy Church!"

I understood, afterwards, that I should have said "to the decisions of the Holy Father." My blunder was huge.

Monseigneur of Grenoble, desirous to know why the prelates he had hired as lawyers had not come, left the room, and remaining alone, I gave testimony of my astonishment to the Cardinal Ferrieri, of the solemn rebellion by Mgr. Fava against the decision of the Holy Father. He said to me:

"What do you want, – *the French Bishops are all Popes!* We are obliged to deal with them so as to avoid a schism. They are not Roman Papists. We put up with them, to avoid a greater evil... Eh! if you knew how much we have to put up with because of them."

To make sense of what follows the story of the Congress, I must mention here that, for several months, two or three good priests, desirous of devoting themselves to the work of the Apostles of the Last Days, lived in community on the first floor of the same palace as us. We had rooms on the second floor, in another wing of the palace. It is quite unnecessary, it seems to me, to say that everything transpired with the blessing of Mgr. Pétagna, of glorious memory. And for two or three years afterwards, I paid the rent for that floor, with subsidies I had received for the foundation of that work for the Mother of GOD.

Those good Fathers lived in retreat, penance, prayer, and sacred study. They came out only for meals. One of those Fathers is still alive: one can consult with him if there is any doubt in anyone's mind. I mentioned nothing about this, nor let the Bishop of Grenoble suspect it, when he came to visit me at Castellammare di Stabia; but I think that old Father Berthier lost no time, while I was speaking with Mgr. Fava, and that he had asked questions of the people of the house, and also other people who in the best of faith would have set him straight. That's why Mgr. Bianchi, when Cardinal Ferrieri had ended the Congress and risen from his seat, said:

"Is it not true, Your Eminence, that one should not cause a schism? I am told that Mélanie has her priests all the while that there are good missionaries on the mountain of La Salette: she pits one altar against the other."

"Oh! no," his Eminence said simply.

And I said:

"I do not believe, Monseigneur, that I pit one altar against another. The Fathers of La Salette are missionaries of La Salette, while those of Italy are missionaries of the Mother of GOD, and they observe her Rule."

"It's bad, it's bad, you must not do like that," said Mgr. Bianchi.

And we separated: the Congress was over.

On exiting, I found my companions again in the antechamber. They told me about the lively insistences made by Father Berthier to attend the Congress, as Mgr. Fava's lawyer; as well as the irritated look on this latter person's face when, on entering, he found none of the Bishops he had invited. Two times he had asked if such and such a Bishop had not arrived. He was told that many Bishops had arrived, but none were allowed to enter. As if furious, he replied:

"I'm the one who told them to come; they had promised; they were bound."

And, addressing himself to the person who had kept the door:

"Perhaps my Bishops did come. Why didn't you let them in?"

"Because I had my orders not to let anyone enter, Your Excellency."

III

As always, Father Berthier came to our hotel to gather information.

The day after, the Bishop of Grenoble sent the Father Berthier to fetch me: His Greatness wanted me to pay a visit to... I don't know exactly whether it was the French College or the French Seminary: wherever it was that the Bishop of Grenoble was lodging, and where women never entered. But Monseigneur always broke the rules.

Father Berthier clearly thought, and in good faith, that given it was He who had come looking for me that I would go out with him by myself. My faithful traveling companions were there to accompany me. We entered the parlor where Mgr. of Grenoble was waiting; and his displeasure, on seeing that I was not alone with Father Berthier, was made manifest to our eyes.

"Eh well," he said to me, "there you are. Wait one moment. I am going to request, of the superior, permission for *you* to enter. Then we will visit the Seminary."

And he disappeared.

During this time I thought:

Monseigneur will not obtain the permission. It seems to me that it is probably here that that Director (or professor) is found who does not believe in La Salette; he causes problems for the seminarists even.

I see Monseigneur returning. By the look on his face, I see that he is not satisfied. He said something in a low voice; then he came to me; then he took me aside, and he asked me what I was going to say to the Pope.

"I don't know anything about it, Monseigneur, for that will depend on the Holy Father to tell me and to ask me."

"But surely you must know something about what the Pope will say to you?"

"No, Monseigneur. I have not yet thought about what the Holy Father will say."

"Ah! you are not very well informed then: you do not know then that the Pope is not just like anybody else; and that you need to think, to prepare what you will say to him."

"Not knowing what the subject will be, nor what the Holy Father will deign to say to me, I cannot possibly think; I abandon myself completely to the good God's holy will."

"Eh! well, listen up. I have here in my hand several banknotes, of one hundred francs each, for **YOUR LITTLE PLEASURES**. If the Pope wanted to make you do something, to everything he says, you

will answer that you will do as the Bishop of Grenoble wants and in whatever way that the Bishop of
Grenoble wants it. And if the Pope told you to go to
such and such a place and do such and such a thing,
you will tell him, "I will go where the Bishop of
Grenoble tells me to go; I want to depend for everything on the Bishop of Grenoble, who is my
VERITABLE SUPERIOR." *And these banknotes are for*
YOUR LITTLE PLEASURES.

I replied:

"Monseigneur, I will tell the Very Holy Father
only what my conscience dictates, at the very moment
that I have the distinguished favor of speaking with
him. Your reasonings are good, Monseigneur, but
they are not mine."

And the Bishop of Grenoble who was offering
banknotes to me (but he always held them on the
hem, on the edge of his wallet), began to put them
away carefully. And we separated. And he no longer
sent anyone to the hotel to gather information or
news.

And on returning to our hotel, my companions
said to me:

"Why did the Bishop of Grenoble hold his
wallet open in his hands for all the time that he was
speaking with you?"

"It is because His Excellency wanted to buy
me. The deal did not succeed: he kept his banknotes,
and I my freedom of conscience."

Since that day, I have never seen the Bishop of Grenoble nor Father Berthier again.

IV

It was, as far as it seems to me, on *December 3*, when I was graced with an audience with the Holy Father Leo XIII.

My two companions had urged me to ask His Holiness the favor of allowing them to kiss his feet. Alas! Alas! the Holy Father's entourage were biased against us!... The Holy Father alone was unaware of the intrigues; and I had spoken about that with His Eminence Cardinal Guidi before my visit with the Holy Father at the Vatican.

The Holy Father received me with kindness and told me in good French:

"Wonderful! you will leave immediately for the mountain of La Salette, with the Rule of the Very Holy Virgin, and you will have it observed by the priests and women religious."

(Those words by the Holy Father confirmed my thinking, that the Holy Father had not yet learnt anything about what had happened at the Congress.)

"Who am I, Very Holy Father, to dare impose myself?"

"Yes, I tell you: You will leave with Monseigneur of Grenoble, and you will ensure that the Rule of the Holy Virgin is observed."

"Very Holy Father, permit me to tell you that those priests and those women religious live a most secular life for a long time now; and that it will be very, very difficult for them to bend to a Rule of humility and abnegation. It seems easier to me to found the Rule using secular clergy of goodwill rather than all those who are currently on the mountain and who are far from being good Christians."

"Listen. You will go up there with the Holy Virgin's Rule, and you will make them familiar with it. And those who do not want to observe it, the Bishop will send them into some other parish."

"Very well, Very Holy Father."

"You will leave then, and leave immediately. But ordinarily when the good God deigns to give a rule of monastic life, he gives, he communicates, to the same person the spirit in which the Rule ought to be observed, that is why you must write it down, when you are in Grenoble, before going back to the mountain of La Salette, and you will send a copy of it to me.

"Oh! Very Holy Father, please do not send me back to Grenoble, under Mgr. Fava; because I will not be free to act."

"How, how is that?"

"Mgr. Fava would order me to write it down as he wishes, not what the Holy Ghost wants."

"But no! no! You will go alone into a room and you will write. When you are done writing your pages, you will send them TO ME."

"Very Holy Father, pardon me if I dare to express to you my difficulties: when I am done writing those pages, Monseigneur of Grenoble will order me to give them to him; and, under the pretext of making them better, he will change everything, while ordering me to copy his explanations on how the Rule of the Holy Virgin is to be practiced."

"Oh! but no. Here is what you will do: when you have written down everything on a sheet of paper, you will put it in an envelope yourself, you will seal it, and you will address it to me like this: **His Holiness the Pope Leo XIII**; that that is me (sic) (while putting his hand on his chest)."

"Very Holy Father, pardon me if again I dare to express the repulsion I feel inside me as to writing under Mgr. of Grenoble's authority. His Greatness will unseal my envelope, he will change what I have written, and he will have his reform copied by another person; to the effect that it will no longer be my words that come to Your Holiness."

"Oh! but no. The Bishop of Grenoble would not act like that!"

"Very Holy Father, I have walked down that path before; the old serpent never sleeps!"

"What to do then?"

"Send me, Very Holy Father, to any other place, provided that I am not under the Bishop of Grenoble's authority."

"Here is what you will do: I have given the order that you go back to the Mountain of La Salette, to
make the priests and women religious there observe
the Rule that the Very Holy Virgin has given to you,
and that, before going back, you will write down the
Constitutions that you will send to me. And you know
that when the Pope has given an order, there's no going back on it."

"Very Holy Father, Our Lord has confided in
you all the power on earth to govern his Church; but
the earth is very wide for all the back and forth go-
ings-on."

"Listen. Pray well this evening; and tomorrow
I will let you know my decision."

"Very Holy Father, I have, in the hall, the
priest whom my holy Bishop of Castellammare has
been kind enough to spare to accompany me on my
trip, and a companion: they would like the favor of
your blessing."

Immediately, the Bishop Camérier, with a
look of annoyance on his face, spoke two words into
the Holy Father's ear, which appeared to be a refusal.
As for myself, having understood, I repeated my request. Finally, the Holy Father asked that they be
made to enter.

V

We returned to the hotel. It was night. In a few words,
I wrote to my Holy Bishop, to wish him a happy Feast

Day. His name is XAVIER.

The day after, we visited His Eminence Cardinal Guidi again, to give him an account of my meeting with the Holy Father; of the bad impression that all His Holiness Pope Leo XIII's entourage gave me; of the difficulties gone through in order for my companions to be blessed by the Holy Father..., and finally of the Holy Father's decision, which was that I should remain in Rome to write, etc., etc.

His Eminence Guidi appeared very surprised and pained that the Holy Father had not received his card with several lines on it that he had addressed to him and sent by his secretary, in order to warn him, to protect against the traps that rebels to the truth of Our Lady of La Salette could lay for him.

"It is unbelievable," said his Eminence, "that they should have stopped my note addressed to the Pope from getting to him. And, however, the person who did that is not ignorant of the trouble, the censure, that any person incurs who permits himself to take possession of a letter coming from a cardinal and addressed to the Pope. It is so true that even a cardinal cannot in any way break the seal of a letter, or an object of another cardinal. What happened to me in my note addressed to the Pope is very serious."

My companions recounted to His Eminence what they had seen before my audience; that is to say, banknotes that Mgr. of Grenoble wanted to give me, on condition that I would not speak to the Holy Father except as he wanted me to speak, him, the Bishop of Grenoble; and that after having been instructed, I had raised my voice protesting to him about it and saying that I would neither speak nor respond to the Holy Father except according to my conscience and what the Divine Master might inspire in me at that moment; then the wrathful look by the Bishop of Grenoble.

I said, among other things, to His Eminence, that I had already begun to write down the Constitutions, the notes being at Castellammare di Stabia; and that I would like to have that notebook; as well as a change of clothes; because I did not know how long it would take me to write. His Eminence, with a paternal good naturedness, said to my companion:

"Go and send back all that Mélanie has need of. And you will have it sent closed up, well sealed, to my address which is this..."

And we all three received his address.

Then His Eminence added:

"Mélanie, take care when you leave the room where you write, to close the door well and to put the key in your pocket, always, always."

On leaving His Eminence's, we went to a stationer's to buy paper, quills, ink, and divers objects, which I put in a scarf.

We returned to our hotel, where we ran into Cardinal Ferrieri accompanied by his Secretary, Mgr. Bianchi. He came to conduct me to the Salésianes, *al monte Palatino*. We entered the hotel and there, alone with the good Cardinal Ferrieri, he renewed on the part of the Holy Father that "His Holiness desires that you should receive nobody, the curiosity of Romans being great; their incessant visits to the visitors' parlor would prevent you from writing. He desires that you should be perfectly free, as much to write letters and seal them yourself as to receive them without their seals having been broken by whomsoever it might be."

Afterwards, we departed.

(I have to say that I had warned my companion that if I saw new wickedness, I would let her know about it in two words, in the Greek language; and that is exactly what happened.)

Along the way, Mgr. Bianchi exhorted me not to let myself be influenced by anyone: that in Rome, one does not believe that I am free to act on my own initiative; and that one always saw me accompanied by those two people, to give me orders. That they have too much influence over me, etc., etc.

"Monseigneur," I responded to him, "Mgr. the Bishop of Grenoble has had proof that I do not let myself be influenced. He has had proof that I do not let myself be bought even, that is to say, I do not sell my freedom of conscience; and without any contempt for his sacred character, I contemn the banknotes he offered me, so that I might repeat to the Holy Father the instructions he had given me. I desire that GOD might illuminate him; that he might enter into the ways of justice; otherwise he will be struck down by lightning by the masters he would have served."

Changing the subject, Mgr. Bianchi said to me, "What are you carrying there, in that packet?"

"Things that I need."

Monseigneur left me. We arrived at the monastery.

His Eminence the Cardinal Ferrieri said to me:

"I have a letter from the Pope for the Community: to present you and recommend you to those good women religious. Among other recommendations, His Holiness tells them that you should have all your freedom, and the freedom of your time."

The parlor door opens. Warmly, I thank His Eminence and I enter.

My first visit was to the Almighty, in his sacrament of love.[110] Then I was led to my cellule, real cellule of a Visitandine, where the doors had no lock. Inside, a small table to write on, two chairs, and a bed. That's it. So I could not secure my writings under lock and key, the sister who had shown me to my cellule having retired to hear the letter from the Holy Father read out loud.

VI

Three or four days later, I received a letter from Father Bernard, missionary of La Salette.

Without elaborating, I will say only that it was a letter full of recriminations: of my "disobedience to the orders of the Pope, etc., etc."

---

[110]sacrament of love: the Holy Eucharist.

I saw therein the influence of Mgr. of Grenoble and Mgr. Bianchi.

I gave thanks to God for having delivered me from their hands. And above all when I understood the manner in which the Bishop of Grenoble wanted to get rid of me, having, in Grenoble, the Father Berthier for his accomplice.

After about seven or eight days, I received the notebook, papers, sealing wax, and a veil from my companion.

Those various things had been carefully packed in a wooden box, addressed to His Eminence the Cardinal Guidi who in addition, before he sent it to me, attached strong red ribbons to the box and sealed it all, at various places, with his wax seal.

It was the Mother Superior who brought the box to me, in broad daylight. Now, it had been opened and gone through, the ribbons cut and the cachets removed. I made a remark to the Mother Superior who humbly replied to me that it had arrived "*as you see it.*"

I had already noticed that the letters I received were opened; and from Castellammare di Stabia, I was made to understand, in a foreign language, that my letters sent to Rome had been opened by Mgr. Bianchi's hirelings in the mail service.

I have to say, so as not to leave any doubt about her, that the Mother Superior, who is innocent and acted in good faith, was not at all complicit in Mgr. Bianchi's and the Bishop of Grenoble's schemes. She was a unknowing tool whom Mgr. Bianchi made use of.

I wrote to Castellammare, and from there one wrote to Cardinal Guidi, who sent a note to the Mother Superior asking whether she had received a superior order that made her act in the way she did. She responded in the negative. He invited her to "follow the Pope's orders."

While waiting, I wrote during the day and for a good part of the night. I was hoping to finish within two months.

Sometimes the Mother Superior came to tell me to go take a walk in the vast garden; other times she told me to keep a sick woman company; one time she told me to visit the caves, the underground chambers beneath Caesar's Palace; and sometimes to come and relax. Mgr. Bianchi, who, doubtless, wanted my sanctification, gave new orders to the Mother Superior. It is pointless to prolong this narrative... Several days before my departure for Castellammare, the Mother Superior, who had already told me that Mgr. Bianchi often came around asking about me, came to make what amounted to apologies to me: "If, sometimes, she had exceeded proper discretion in my regards..." I hugged her with affection, assuring her that she had always treated me with great kindness. She opened up to me: among other things, she said this:

"The Holy Father sent, about three times, the Cardinal Ferrieri, to know whether you were writing; if anyone had come to visit you, and if it was not too much pressure on you being locked up. His Eminence appears to greatly esteem you. He asked me about your health; he encouraged me to take care of you. Mgr. Bianchi came, very often, to ask a lot of things about you as to your conduct in the Community. He seemed highly irritated when I spoke highly of you; and he reproached me for not making you practice the virtues. He had ordered me to keep all your letters, and also those that had been addressed to you; and, so that you might not see that they had been opened, to return them in the evening, when you were in the refectory. He commanded me to humiliate you, above all in public; to upset you, to contradict you in everything: 'Make her attend services.' And lastly he told me: 'See to it that she does not hold court with any individuals who visit the Monastery. When she associates with the women religious, push her away, tell her to go where people of society are admitted. Do not let her keep the candle burning at night for more than an hour.'"

Once I had finished my writings, I had them carried to Cardinal Ferrier for the Holy Father, as well as my letter addressed to the Pope, in which I told him that I was at His Holiness' disposition, to go where he would say I needed to go.

Fifteen days passed and I still had no news. A month passed, nothing. But Mgr. Bianchi came in those latter days. I learnt about it through the Mother Superior's zeal. This time they wanted to make me into a Visitandine, they wanted to cloister me. I had already received that news from a French priest, to whom Mgr. Fava had written: "Finally, she is locked up in a cloister, where she will never leave again!"

They had not counted on the Almighty. It is true that one tried everything and anything possible and impossible. I wrote again to the Holy Father who probably never received my letters.

I fall ill: I keep to bed for several days only; but the battles bravely continued. The Mother Superior was young, the oldest women religious were at their ease with her. That is why, when the Mother Superior entered with me in recreation, one sister said:

"Mother, Mélanie is too week to come here. Look at her, she looks like death warmed over."

And seeing that the Mother Superior wasn't paying any attention, she said:

"Mother, they entrusted Mélanie to us in good health, and now look at her!"

Another day, the same sister said to her:

"I would really love it if Mélanie stayed with us for a long time, and even forever; but not at the expense of her life; and you know how we were told to take good care of her. It's a duty of conscience to warn the Holy Father of the danger she's running."

While waiting, the battle intensified. And to make matters worse, letters from the city arrived for me, wherein I was accused of disobedience, stubbornness, being rebellious to the will of the head of the Church, and almost a damned soul!!!

Meanwhile, the Mother Superior came to tell me, that it was not proper for me to be without a veil on in the house; given the sisters wore one. I immediately put a veil over my head which I never took off again. Then she insinuated that I should be a Visitandine. I told her that the Holy Father Pius IX had said to my holy Bishop that in order "to complete my mission, I cannot be cloistered." On another occasion, the Sister Placide said to the Mother Superior:

"Mother, God be my witness, for my peace of conscience, I am relinquishing the responsibility that the Community has accepted to take care of Mélanie, to leave her care to you entirely: because it is not for us to be giving orders to Mélanie, it is for the people who have entrusted her to us."

"I have written," said the Mother Superior, "I have written two times."

Finally, Cardinal Ferrieri arrived; and among other things, he said to me that the Holy Father decided that I should return to Castellammare: and that I could write so that someone might come and fetch me. Which is what happened.

VII

As I was in route, outside the convent, I asked my companion if there were still in Castellammare believers in the divine Message.

"Yes," she replied, "but in Rome, Mgr. Fava, Mgr. Bianchi, and Father Berthier have not stopped disseminating criminal calumnies and errors [about you] everywhere."

"What is said against me," I replied, "my sins

justify them; it is an exercise of patience in order to better prepare me to enter into my nullity. As for the divine Message, it will crush the Almighty's enemies. Does not GOD say, through Jeremiah's mouth, that speech is an ardent fire and a hammer that breaks rocks? That is why, he who rises up against the word of GOD does nothing else than become the means for spreading his word even more widely."

At that moment the good Father Trévis arrived, who came to meet us. Among other things, I said to him:

"Before quitting Rome, I would like to see the new statue of Our Lady of La Salette, which Mgr. Fava had commissioned."

We went there.

On entering the workshops, we came across diverse rough-hewn statues. One only was finished. But none of them appeared to represent a Virgin in any way, shape, or form. I said to Father Trévis:

"But where is the statue then, based on Mgr. of Grenoble's model?"

"Here it is," said the gentleman who was giving us a tour of the workshop.

"But no! but no! Sir; that cannot be Our Lady of La Salette! It does not resemble her in the least."

"Nonetheless," said the gentleman, "it is made exactly according to the model that you see behind it, and which the Bishop of Grenoble gave to me. Besides, he must be well-informed, being the Bishop of the diocese where the Apparition took place."

"His Greatness, Mgr. Fava, yes, ought to be well-informed; but the fact of the matter is that he has never interrogated either of the two shepherds. His model then is a complete fantasy: and it is with good reason that you can put on his statue's plinth these words: '**Statue of Mgr. Fava's private vision!**' It will never be the statue of Our Lady of La Salette, whose hair was not seen, and who wore a large cross on her chest. The Madonna, *per caritas*, by compassion, *came to teach us through words and by example.* One day GOD will avenge the contempt done to his divine Mother!"

We withdrew. The gentleman, in a low voice, asked M. Trévis, "who is that lady who seems so informed as to Our Lady of La Salette's costume?"

Given I was about to leave Rome that evening, M. Trévis told him:

"She is the Shepherdess of La Salette..."

We went back to the hotel, and from there to the train station for Naples. It is then that Father Trévis and my companion spoke about the intrigues, the calumnies that Messeigneurs Bianchi and Fava, and Father Berthier had spread throughout Rome and in France by written document. None of that affected me: it was all to my benefit. What deeply distressed me though was the false statue in marble ordered by the Bishop of Grenoble and which was supposed to be crowned that same year of 1879 on the Mountain of La Salette!!!

My GOD! Do not permit the Bishop of Grenoble and Father Berthier's error to triumph! You, for
whom nothing is impossible, stop the vain plots of the
enemies of truth. Have pity on your people; have pity
on the blindness of many of your anointed; convert us
all to you, Lord JESUS!

In the evening, we took the train for Naples-
Castellammare di Stabia, and it was during that trip
that my companions informed me about the new war
that hostile newspapers were waging against the divine Apparition, which said:

"That on shedding abundant tears, during my
visit with the Holy Father, I had declared to him that I
had seen nothing on the Mountain";

Which said:

"That the Pope does not believe in the Apparition; and that it is for this reason that *the Pope* is having a statue made that will not represent Our Lady of
La Salette";

Which said:

"The Pope no longer wishes to put the children before the statues of Our Lady of La Salette";

Which said:

"Mélanie did not wish to obey the Pope; she
was excommunicated";

Which said:

"The Pope imprisoned Mélanie in Rome. She
makes a fuss. She wants to exit, and the Pope does

not want her to exit, etc. etc."

VIII

Here we are back in Castellammare. A great sadness grips my heart. I no longer find Monseigneur Petagna, my holy Bishop.

He had left his exile here on earth several months earlier; he had gone to receive the noble and sublime recompense that GOD reserves for the most worthy Ministers, for those who have fought the good fight for justice.

Several months later, the newspapers and other printed material inundated the news from every quarter, announcing with pomp: "*the crowning of the statue in beautiful white marble, executed under the direction of the Sovereign Pontiff, according to the model that Monseigneur Fava had given him!!*"

Meanwhile, I received a letter from Rome, and on the following day I received many more from diverse people, including those from Rome, all which said nearly the same thing:

"I do not know, dear Sister, if you have heard the news that is running through Rome? It says that, ever since last May, the new statue commissioned by Mgr. of Grenoble has not been executed on: because the sculptor has been afflicted with an infirmity of the arm."

Another letter said this:

"Did you know, my very dear Sister, that the sculptor of the Virgin by Monseigneur Fava has been struck with paralysis in his arm?"

Another:

"We have just learnt that the crowning of Our Lady of La Salette will not take place this year because of an accident that happened to the Master sculptor, who has a paralysis in his arms: he was unable to finish his work on time. Or, if the crowning takes place, it will be that of the model in chalk (plaster), while waiting for the statute in marble to be completed..."

What is **true** is that in September 1879, the model (**in plaster**!) of Mgr. Fava was crowned **with great pomp**: because the reproduction in marble was unable to be brought to completion. The real reason not being given.

From various quarters, I am written to, asking for information, and I hear the news that is circulating France, and which was originated by Mgr. Fava and Father Berthier. Sometimes it is that the "sculptor must have run off." Other times it is that "he is too exhausted. He was ordered to take some time off to rest, etc., etc."

But in my dear mountainous region, where the newspapers do not reach, the nearest railroad stop being more than four hours away, one does not know what the Fathers of La Salette say, that is, "The statue in white marble will be very verisimilitudinous: a work of art.[111] The model was made by His Greatness Mgr. the Bishop of Grenoble; and based on that marvelous model, the statue will be executed in Rome, *under the direction* of the great Pope Leo XIII. The Shepherds were unable to provide guidance on the Virgin's costume. Our great Bishop Mgr. Fava knew better, and he was able to give the exact rendering of that Heavenly costume in his model, which is ravishing in beauty."[112]

On the day of coronation, the crowds came in mass. I leave the description of it to an ocular witness who recounted the event to me:

"The Basilica was adorned. The new statue brought from Rome was on the Main Altar; but hidden behind a curtain. Everyone was filled with desire to see the *true* Our Lady of La Salette. Those who found themselves at the back of the Basilica stood on their chairs in order to get a first glimpse of it. The ceremony was deemed too long. Finally one heard a loud noise. It was the crowd who said that the curtain seemed to be moving. Finally, the curtain was lowered. At first, only the head was seen, when the inhabitants of our regions exclaimed:

"'That's not right! that's not Her! She has her hair falling down over her shoulders!'

---

[111]Original footnote: The *work of art* is of an incomprehensible asininity and ugliness for whomsoever might not be aware of the profound aesthetic unintelligence of modern Christians.

[112]Original footnote: One must be a missionary of La Salette or an editor of the *Cross* to write such an advertisement, wherein ALL *the words* are ridiculous.

"The curtain continued to drop; as they saw more of her distinctly, they said with astonishment:

"'Oh! that is not Our Lady of La Salette: she has no Cross!'

"'Oh! her hands are visible and she wears a coat like some of the girls in Paris: it's not Her, it's not Her.'

"And there was a general disapprobation; until the chanting drowned out the murmurs of that good people."[113]

I respond here to two requests that were often made of me:

First, why are the Medals and the Images rep-

---

[113]Original footnote: The cardinal Guibert, delegate of Leo XIII, not wishing, because of his great age, to mount the stairs of the temporary altar, a missionary took the diadem and placed it himself on the head of the plaster statue. They put it on the scrap heap when the statue in marble was completed. Which of the two was crowned? Neither. First of all, the Holy Father does not crown a statue in plaster. Second, it is essential that the crown be placed by the delegate: he can be assisted, but he must be physically present in the act. Third, the statue must be what will be honored.

The decree to crown Our Lady of Salette was not then executed! When one executes it, one will crown the true statue of the Apparition. Mélanie's prayer: "My God, do not permit the Bishop of Grenoble and Father Berthier's error to triumph, etc." could not be more completely answered. Everything was missing, *even the Discourse*. Mgr. Paulinier who should have pronounced it was found to be exhausted, Mgr. Fava READ tirades against the Free Masons. Even the *procession* could not be executed. No order in that discontented crowd. – No miracle had been granted to the prayers made before that statue. Mélanie had said: "The falsely crowned statue will never grant miracles."

resenting Our Lady of La Salette not distributed all over France, as all other medals and miraculous images are ordinarily?

Second, why aren't the medals or images of Our Lady of Salette available for purchase from any of the merchants of pious objects?

I asked myself the same things; and I suffered because of it. I would have liked to purchase them, to spread the devotion of that sweet Mother everywhere I went. It was only in 1871 that I discovered the old serpent's trick.

I had come back to France to see my mother who I missed; then to Lyon, to see one of my sisters. After having gone to Fourvières, we entered into nearly every shop of objects of piety, without being able to find a single medal or image of La Salette!...

Then, I said to my sister:

"Do you know where those medals are struck?"

"Yes," she said.

"Bring me there."

We arrived, and I asked for five or six medals wholesale. The patroness told me that she no longer had any.

"How is that?" I said to her. "Isn't this the place where the medals are struck that are sold on the mountain of La Salette?"

"Yes," that lady said to me, "but the missionaries gave us the business, with the condition that every other merchant of objects of piety shall be **excluded**. You can find the medals for purchase from the Fathers of La Salette."

That is how I found out, my heart filled with sadness, why the medals of Our Lady of Salette could not be found in other shops.

Is it not the case that those poor miserable Fathers have lost sight of the Almighty, their soul, the eternity of suffering, in order to substitute their glory, their material gain, for the glory of that God who must judge them?... oh!... oh!... what have we become!... And those beings dare to call themselves the Missionaries of La Salette, while their entire preoccupation was to sock away treasures upon treasures, and they hate the poor! They let the good, the disinterested, the virtuous Maximin go hungry, which would have made the very stones weep with compassion!

Sister Mary of the Cross, Shepherdess of La Salette.

Certified copy, May 18, 1904.

H. RIGAUX

Curate d'ARGŒUVES.

Appendix 2: Apparition of the Very Holy Virgin on the Mountain of La Salette

The notes that follow, which form a commentary on the preceding story made by the Shepherdess, are in the hand of an excellent priest who had the honor of knowing Mélanie personally and of being her director of conscience in the last period of her life.

THE APPARITION

OF THE

VERY HOLY VIRGIN
ON THE MOUNTAIN OF LA SALETTE
September 19, 1846.

Published by the Shepherdess of La Salette with the Imprimatur of Mgr. the BISHOP OF LECCE.

"Ah, well! my children, you will pass it on to all my people."

I

On September 18, the eve of the holy Apparition of the Holy Virgin, I was alone, as usual, watching my

Masters' four animals. Around eleven o'clock in the morning, I saw coming towards me a small boy. On seeing him, I grew afraid, because it seemed to me that everyone ought to know that I ran away from all sorts of company. That child approached me and said to me, "Little girl, I'm going to join you, I too am from Corps." On these words, my bad nature immediately showed itself, and, taking several steps backward, I said to him, "I don't want anyone, I want to be alone." Then, I walked away, but that child followed me,[114] saying to me, "Come on, let me come with you, my Master told me to come and watch over my animals with yours, I am from Corps."

I walked away from him, indicating to him that I wanted to be alone; and after having walked away, I sat down on the grass. There, I held my conversation with the small flowers of the Good God.

One moment later, I look behind me and I see Maximin sitting very close by. He immediately says, "You'll see, I will be very good."[115] But my bad nature would not listen to reason. I got up off the grass

---

[114]Original footnote: Mélanie was fourteen years and ten months old then, but was neither tall nor strong, she appeared barely ten years old. She was very timid by temperament, and her long years of service among strangers, as well as the lack of tenderness on the part of her mother *who had never embraced her*, had done nothing to reform that defect of character. But the pious child, whom Heaven had visited a long time before 1846, sought solitude above all in order to be one with GOD. Her "Dear Brother" said to her, "Sister, run away from the noise of the world, love retreat and meditation; focus your heart on the Cross and keep the Cross in your heart; so that Jesus Chris might be your only occupation. Love silence and you will hear the voice of GOD in Heaven who will speak to you in your heart; keep company with yourself and GOD will be all yours."

precipitously, and I ran farther away without saying a word to him, and I started again to play with the flowers of the Good God. A moment later, Maximin was there also, telling me that he would be good, and that he would not speak, and that he was bored being all alone, and that his Master sent him to be with me... etc. This time, I had pity on him, and I made him a sign to sit down, and I continued to play with the little flowers of the Good God.

It did not take long before Maximin broke the silence; he begins laughing (I think he was mocking me); I look at him and he says, "Let's have some fun, lets play a game." I said nothing to him in response, for I was so ignorant that I understood nothing about playing a game with another person, having always kept to myself. I amused myself with the flowers, and Maximin coming very close to me did nothing but laugh, saying that the flowers did not have ears to hear me, and that we should play together. But I had no desire to play the game he said he wanted to play.

---

[115]Original footnote: Maximin was only eleven years old and acted about three years younger. He had never worked before, and his father, a wheelwright in Corps, had been asked if his son could replace, for one week, a shepherd who was ill. The father refused at first, saying that "Mémin," stupid as he was, would let the animals fall off the cliffs; he had given in on the promise that there would always be someone to watch over him. "Mémin" was as candid as he was lively, indiscreet and also naughty: "Just watch me, I will be very good," – what simplicity! But he was always turbulent and in perpetual motion; and although very intelligent, he was so inattentive that in three years time his father had barely been able to teach him "Our Father" and "Hail Mary"; he called him "innocent."

Mélanie did not know nor understand French. Maximin did not speak it either, but he could understand *some words of it*.

However, I began to speak with him, and he told me that the ten days he was supposed to spend with his Master were about to come to an end, and that then he would return to Corps to be with his father, etc...

While he was speaking to me, the church bell of La Salette could be heard ringing, it was the Angelus; I made a sign to Maximin to lift his soul up to God. He uncovered his head and kept silent for a moment. Then I said to him, "Do you want to eat?" "Yes," he said, "let's." We sat down together; I took out of my sack some provisions that my Masters had given to me, and according to my habitude, before cutting into my small round loaf of bread, and with the point of the knife, I made a cross in my bread, and in the middle a very small hole, saying, "If the devil is here, would that he might come out, and if the good God is here, would that he might remain" and quickly, quickly I covered the hole again. Maximin burst out laughing loudly, and kicked my piece of bread with his foot, which flew out of my hands, rolled down the side of the mountain, and was lost.

I had another piece of bread, we ate it together; then we played a game; then, understanding that Maximin ought to have need of something more to eat,[116] I indicated to him a place on the mountain that was covered with little fruit. I encouraged him to go

---

[116]Original footnote: Instead of scolding the scatterbrain who, with an agile kick, had made the first small loaf of bread roll down the mountain, not only does she share with him the second loaf of bread, but she thinks only of the need he must have to eat, and does not think of herself. The privations, the penances that that frail child imposed on herself for years, and that she continued all throughout her life, were more than heroic: they were miraculous.

and eat some of it, which he soon did: he ate some and brought back a hatful of them. In the evening, we went down the mountain together, and we promised to return to watch our animals together.

On the following day, September 19,[117] I find myself on the path with Maximin again; we climbed the mountain together. I found Maximin to be very good, very simple, and that he willingly spoke about what I wished to speak about; he was also very flexible, not keeping rigidly to his own thoughts or feelings; he was a little curious moreover, for when I distanced myself from him, when he saw that I had stopped, he quickly ran over to see what I was doing and to hear what I was saying to the flowers of the Good God; and if he did not arrive in time, he asked me what I had said. Maximin asked me to teach him a game. The morning was already quite advanced: I told him to gather flowers to make a "Paradise."[118]

We both went to work; soon we had a quantity of flowers of diverse colors. In the village, the Angelus could be heard ringing, for the sky was gor-

---

[117]Original footnote: September 19, that same year, turned out to be the eve of the feast of Our Lady of Seven Sorrows, which the Church recited the first Vespers of at the very hour of the Apparition. The Holy Virgin's discourse, her clothing, her tears, the path she took, which has exactly the sinuosities of that of Calvary, all were in correspondence with that feast, so that we have no doubt that our revolts against GOD and his Church were the seven swords that, at the foot of the Cross, transpierced his heart.

[118]The scatterbrain, who spent all his time in Corps in amusements for his age, grows bored as he did the day before and asks again to play. The Shepherdess, who had never played before, taught him then how to make a "Paradise"!...

geous, there were no clouds. After telling the Good God what we knew, I told Maximin that we should lead our animals to a small plateau near a gully, where there would be stones with which to build the "Paradise." We led our animals to the designated place, and then we took our small meal; then we began to carry stones and to construct our little house, which consisted of a ground floor, which we called our habitation, then a floor above it which was, according to us, "Paradise."

The upper floor was garnished with flowers of various colors, with wreaths suspended by the stems of flowers. That "Paradise" was covered by one large rock that we had covered with flowers; we had also suspended wreaths all around it. With "Paradise" built, we looked at it; we grew sleepy; we stretched out on the grass there about two paces away, and we took a nap.

The Beautiful Lady was sitting on our "Par-

MARY had brought together these two dear children, of such opposite character, and the hand of her providence knew how to lead "the innocent" onto the mountain in so natural a way that the shepherd who Maximin replaced, on the day after the Apparition was healed and resumed his job, and said with charming ingenuity: "I really had bad luck!" – "How is that?" someone asked. – "I fell ill: if it wasn't for that I would have seen the Holy Virgin! It is me whom *Mémin* replaced... Then, it was that same week exactly that he saw the Holy Virgin. Ah! Sir, without that illness, *it is me who should have seen* the Holy Virgin!"

That young man was sweet, gentle, and pious. But the Mother of GOD had need of a good scatterbrain, like Maximin, who saw *nothing* in the Apparition, and who was *not aware* of himself even.

adise" without it crushing it.[119]

II

Having reawakened, and not seeing our animals, I called Maximin and I climbed up the hillock. From there, having seen that our animals were lying down tranquilly, I went back down and Maximin was going up when, all of a sudden, I saw a beautiful light, brighter than the sun, and I could barely let out these words: "Maximin, do you see that, over there? Ah! my God!" At the same time I dropped the stick I was holding. I do not know what delicious thing passed through me at that moment, but I felt attracted to it; I felt a great deal of respect full of love, and my heart wanted to run faster than I could.[120]

I looked very firmly at that light which was not moving, and as if it had opened up I apperceived another light much more brilliant and which was moving, and in that light a Very Beautiful Lady was seated on our "Paradise," holding her head in her hands. That Beautiful Lady got up, she crossed her

[119]Original footnote: As it was not yet a question of the Beautiful Lady, Mélanie's eagerness to pay attention to that particularity denotes her admiration for the Holy Virgin's goodness, who in that way testified to her approval of their little recreation.

[120]Original footnote: The first feeling that Maximin had, who had never experienced an apparition before and believed that Mélanie was afraid, was different. "Go," he said, "pick up your stick" and brandishing his he menaced: "if she touches us, I will let her *have it*!" Already the light opened up and Mélanie immediately recognized the Holy Virgin and was seized with fear, almost panic stricken, to see the Holy Virgin weeping, whom she had never before seen except in her beatitude."

arms mildly while looking at us, and she said: "*Come closer, my children, do not be afraid; I am here to announce the great news to you.*" Those sweet and gentle words made me fly to her, and my heart would have wanted to bind to her forever. Having come really close to the Beautiful Lady, before her, on her right, she begins her discourse, and tears began also to flow from her beautiful eyes:

If my people do not want to submit, I will be forced to let the hand of my Son go. It is so heavy and so weighty that I can no longer hold it back.

For all the time that I've spent suffering for you all! If I do not want my Son to abandon you, I am charged with praying to him non-stop. And as for you others, you do not care. No matter how much you pray, how much you do, you can never repay me for the amount of trouble I have gone to for you.

I have given you six days to work, I have reserved the seventh day for myself, and one does not grant it to me.[121] *It is what makes my Son's arm so heavy.*

Those who led the ox carts do not know how to speak without putting my Son's Name in the middle of it. Those are the two things that weigh down my Son's arm so much.[122]

If the harvest is spoilt, it is on account of you all.

---

[121]The Holy Virgin speaks here in the name of the Lord, and *the* LIVING CHRIST whom she carries in her heart pronounced the words at the same moment.

I showed it to you last year with the pota-toes;[123] you did not pay any attention; just the oppo-site: when you found spoilt ones, you swore and you invoked my Son's Name in vain. They will continue to spoil; at Christmastime, there will no longer be any.

Here, I tried to interpret the word "potatoes"; I believe what was meant were apples. The Beautiful and Good Lady, divining my thought, replied also:

Do you not understand, my children? I will say it in another way.

The translation in French reads like this:

If the harvest is spoilt, it is your fault alone; I pointed it out to you last year with the potatoes, and you thought it no big deal; on the contrary, when you found the spoilt ones, you swore and you used the Son's Name in vain. They will continue to spoil, and

---

[122]In absence of the observation of Sunday, there cannot be a religious life. Here it is fifteen centuries already after Tertullian repeated those words to the faithful of his day: "Without Sunday there can be no Christians. *Non est christianus sine dominica*." Also, among the questions addressed by persecutors to the martyrs, one distinguished above all this: "Do you observe Sunday?" and on their affirmative response, that was enough, they recognized thereby Christianity part and parcel so to speak. But the Holy Virgin reproaches her people of a second crime, more enormous even than the violation of Sunday, it is Blasphemy. When every mouth not only does not pray, but blasphemes; when an entire people, as in France, not only forgets to honor GOD, but insults him and repudiates him, what punishments are not merited? "*Those are the two things that so greatly weigh my Son's arm down.*"

[123]potatoes: the Irish Potato Famine began in 1845; there was also a lesser known, at least today, corresponding European Potato Famine at around the same time.

at Christmas, there will be no more.

If you have wheat, you must not seed it.

Everything you seed, the beasts will eat it; and what does grow will fall away like powder when you try to thrash it. There will be a great famine. Before the famine comes, small children under seven will take to trembling and die in the arms of the people who hold them; others will do penance by hunger. The nuts will go bad; the grapes will rot.[124]

Here, the Beautiful Lady who was ravishing me rested for a moment without making herself heard; I saw however that she continued amiably to move her kind lips, for she was speaking. Maximin

---

[124]Original footnote: These threats were conditional: "*If my people do not want to submit.*" The act of conversion produced after the Apparition was not sufficient: the majority of the threats were realized to the letter.

The Holy Virgin had said that the potatoes would continue to go bad and that at Christmastime there would be no more. Now, from the beginning of winter, poor people would die of hunger on the mountain: they had only potatoes to eat. It was like that in all of France and abroad, but particularly in Ireland. All the newspapers of London from January 21, 1847 reported on it: "The resulting loss, for Ireland alone, from the lack of the potato harvests, may be equal to 12 million pounds sterling, or 300 million francs." (*Gazette du Midi*, January 28, 1847.) That scarcity having continued for many years, the population of that Island dropped in 1866-1867, from eight million to five million. Those three million Irish either died of famine or emigrated...

She had said that the wheat would be eaten by the beasts and would fall to dust. Consequently, the "grain" blight was declared in 1851 and caused enormous losses in Europe.

Here is what a correspondent of *l'Univers* wrote, on that wheat blight, in the July 15, 1856 issue:

was receiving his secret at that time. Then, addressing herself to me, the Very Holy Virgin spoke to me and gave me a secret in French. Here is that secret, in its entirety, just as she gave it to me:

III

1. Mélanie, what I am about to tell you now will not always be your secret; you can publish it

---

"I opened the alveoli or withered straw [sic]. The former had no grain inside, they were clearly what had been invaded first, and when the embryos were barely hatched. The latter enclosed a withered and desiccated grain that provides no nourishment; these are what were invaded later. In both the former and the latter we found, in the form of a dry powder, small worms which, doubtless, produced these ravages. Anyone can, today, confirm the same phenomenon: it is enough to grab the first blade of wheat, to take the spikes in hand, to open the corollas tainted at their root with a black mark, and one will see the animalcules pullulating."

She had said that a great famine would come and that men would make penance for hunger. Now, in 1854-1855, the wheat in France sold for 55 and 60 francs per one hundred kilograms. After statistics published by the *Constitutionel* and *l'Univers* in 1856, the high price of victuals would have caused in France, for the two years 1854 and 1855, the death of one hundred fifty-two thousand people; and more than one million for all of Europe, according to some newspapers. And *l'Univers* on December 12, 1856, added: "Under that euphemism 'Decease resulting from high prices,' one must read: 'Deaths due to poverty and famine'... One does not know the figure for 1856 yet, but the cause has not gone away..."

In Spain, the government bought wheat for sixty million royals, in order to avoid a shortage. In Poland, provisions were so dear in 1856 that the Russian emperor raised the wages of functionaries by a third.

in 1858. [125]

2. *The priests, my Son's ministers, the priests, by*
    the bad life they lead, by their irreverences
    and by their impiety while celebrating the
    holy mysteries, by their love for money, love
    for honor and pleasures, the priests have be-
    come cesspools of impurity. Yes, the priests

_____

She had said that before the famine, small children
would begin trembling and die in the arms of the people who held
them. Now, in 1847, the realization of that threat began with a
large mortality of small children in the canton of Corps. In 1854,
in France, seventy-five thousand children under seven years old
died of the sweats. A glacial cold seized them, followed by a
trembling that led to death after two hours of suffering.

She had said that the nuts would go bad. Now, a report
addressed to the minister of the interior in 1852 confirmed that
the blight on nuts had weakened the harvest the year before, in
Lyonnais, Beaujolais, and Isère; and that it was a calamity for
those regions, whose harvest of nuts is one of the main
resources.

She had said that the grapes would rot. Now the
scourge continues still. Soon it will be sixty years since the
grapes turn rotten.

The fulfillment only of prophetic public threats, – is it not
enough to make one say: If La Salette is not an article of faith, it
is an article of good faith; if La Salette is not a dogma, it is an
immense grace which some have not profited enough by?

By commenting on and meditating on the Secret, verse
by verse, we will see that the prophetic menaces, more
numerous and much graver than those of the public discourse,
have been plainly realized to this day. It is the divine flame par
excellence, for the prophesy is not possible except by GOD. It is
evident that it is above the strength of creatures not only to
control the distant events, but also to foresee them with certitude
when their causes do not yet exist.

demand vengeance, and vengeance is sus-
pended over their heads. Woe unto the priests
and to the people consecrated to God who, by
their infidelities and their bad life, crucify my
Son once again! The sins of the people conse-
crated to God cry out to Heaven and call
down a vengeance, and behold how the
vengeance is at their door, for there is no one

The great Apparition of La Salette has had the light of all the flames shed on it. Three years and some months afterwards, M. the abbot Michel Perrin, who served at the shrine, attested to, proof in hand, *more than two hundred fifty healings* obtained by invocation to Our Lady of La Salette. The fountain, which did not "flow" except on the melting of the snows, or as a result of great rains, and which, since then, resists all drying up, is a permanent miracle.

Divine flame, interrogations that the [two] children were made to endure. Was it not miraculous to see two children who, the day before, did not speak French, utter long conversations in French without understanding it, and explain themselves in that language? "The most subtle interrogations do not frighten them at all, the most specious phrases do not disconcert them at all; they escape all traps by means of clear and peremptory responses. Confronted or separated, their dispositions harmonize, complete, corroborate, and that on the most insignificant of details. Theologians have admitted defeat; jurisconsults and scholars, at first of an extreme boldness, are soon afraid to have seen all too clearly. After one of those interrogations, one of them said to Mélanie:

'My child, aren't you tired of repeating so often the same things?'

'No, sir.'

'That ought to bother you though, above all when one asks you awkward questions?'

'Sir, *no one has ever put awkward questions to me...*'"

anymore to implore mercy and pardon for the people; there are no more generous souls, there is no one worthy to offer as the immaculate Victim to the Eternal, in favor of the world.

3. *God will strike in an unprecedented manner.*

4. *Woe unto the inhabitants on earth! God will exhaust his anger, and no one will be able to escape from so many combined troubles.*

5. *The chiefs, the leaders of the people of God, have neglected prayer and penance, and the demon has clouded their intelligences; they have become those wandering stars that the*

Silence and stupefaction! All the audience looks at each other, and each one is *very discomfited* after having spent so much energy in vain.

The abbot Dupanloup, who became bishop of Orleans, admitted having been *beaten* by those two children. "It is important to note," he wrote on June 11, 1848, "that never have the accused, in justice, been pursued by questions on a crime, as those two poor little rustic children have been for two years, over the vision that they recount. To some difficulties often prepared in advance, sometimes longly and insidiously premeditated, they have always replied promptly, in a brief, clear, precise, peremptory manner. One feels that they would be radically incapable of such presence of mind, if all that they said was not the truth. One has seen them led, as one would lead evildoers, to the place itself of their revelation or their imposture; the most distinguished and grave individuals did not disconcert them, nor did threats or injuries frighten them, nor did caresses or gentleness make them bend, nor did the longest interrogations fatigue them, nor did the frequent repetition of all those tests find them in contradiction, either singly or together."

That supernatural assistance lasted all their life.

> *old devil will drag around by his tail in order*
> *to make them perish. God will permit the old*
> *serpent to sow divisions among rulers, in all*
> *societies, and in all families; one will suffer*
> *physical and mental anguish; God will aban-*
> *don them to themselves and will send punish-*
> *ments that will continue for more than thirty-*
> *five years.*

A knowledgable professor of theology and his friend, the curate of a large city, had come to La Salette with a dozen objections prepared and studied in advance, to propose to Maximin after he had left his booth to go and tell, at the request of pilgrims (who preferred him to the Missionaries), the story of the miracle. When Maximin had completed his recitation, the professor put forward the first objection. Maximin limited himself to saying: "Pass to the second"; the same thing happened with the 2nd, 3rd, 4th, and 5th objection; Maximin responded then in a few words; he destroyed the first five objections, and with them the remaining seven. On seeing that, that professor and that curate told us the same thing, for we were standing beside them: "This young man is always in his mission; he is assisted by the Holy Virgin today as on the first days; it is evident to us. No theologian, were he the most knowledgeable in the world, could have pulled off such a *tour de force*. All that is certainly superhuman. He has proven the miracle to us better than the strongest of demonstrations could do." (Aug. Nicolas.)

All these divine signs count for nothing next to the marvels of grace operated on souls. To convert sinners, to bring them back to Jesus, such is the goal of the apparition of La Salette and such was the effect everywhere where she was understood. Was it not miraculous to see converted, on the children's recitation, crowds who received them with the ultimate prejudice at first and very often with contempt? From the first year, the canon of Corps was entirely renewed. Not only did nobody blaspheme anymore, not only did nobody work on Sunday, but everyone frequented church and, from 1847, almost everyone went to Easter mass. Thus in Corps, with a population of 1800 inhabitants, there were not thirty people who neglected that important duty.

6. *Society is on the eve of the most terrible scourges and the greatest of events; one should expect to be governed by an iron rod and to drink from the chalice of God's anger.*

7. *That the Vicar of my Son, the Sovereign Pontiff Pius IX should not leave Rome any longer, after the year 1859; but that he should remain firm and generous, that he should fight with the arms of faith and love; I will be with him.*

8. *That Napoleon should be distrusted; his heart is duplicitous, and when he wants to be both Pope and emperor, God will soon leave him; he is that eagle that, always wanting to rise, will fall on the sword that he had wished to use to oblige the people to [help him] rise up.*

9. *Italy will be punished for its ambition in wanting to shake off the yoke of the Lord of Lords; it will also be given to war; blood will flow from all sides; churches will be closed or profaned; priests, men religious, will be chased out; one will make them die, and die a cruel death. Many will abandon the faith, and the number of priests and men religious who sep-*

But why go on about these important signs when each one of us can cite a superior authority: that of the Holy Church. If La Salette is not an article of faith, it is an article of good faith; if it is not a dogma, it is a grace that nobody has benefited enough by.

[125]Original footnote: Admirable delay! The Holy Virgin wanted Mélanie released from her Secret, immediately *after* her Apparition in Lourdes, on February 11, 1858! It is surprising that no one has seemed to noticed that (LÉON BLOY).

arate from the true religion will be great; even Bishops will be found amongst them.

10. That the Pope should be on the alert against makers of miracles, for the time has come when the most surprising prodigies will take place on earth and in the air.

11. In the year 1864, Lucifer, with a large number of demons will be detached from hell: they will abolish the faith little by little and even among the people consecrated to God; they will blind them in a certain way, so that at least with a particular grace those people will assume the spirit of those bad angels; more religious orders will lose their faith entirely and will lose many souls.

12. Bad books will abound on earth, and the spirits of darkness will extend a universal relaxation everywhere for everything that concerns the service of God; they will have a very great power over nature; there will be churches to serve those spirits. People will be transported from one place to another by those bad spirits, and even priests because they will not be led by the good spirit of the Gospel, which is a spirit of humility, charity, and zeal for the glory of God. They will resurrect the dead and the just (that is to say that those decedents will look like just souls who had lived on earth, in order to better seduce men; those so-called resurrected decedents, who will be none other than the demon under those exteriors, will preach another Gospel contrary to that of the real Christ Jesus, denying Heaven's existence as well even as the souls of the damned. All those souls will appear as if united in body.) There will be everywhere extraordinary prodigies, because the true faith has dried up and a false light will shine on the world. Woe unto the Princes of the Church who will be occupied only with socking away riches upon riches, with safeguarding only their authority and dominating with pride.

13. My Son's Vicar will have a great deal to suffer because, for a time, the Church will be abandoned to great persecutions; this will be the time of darkness; the Church will have a terrible crisis on its hands.

14. The holy faith in God having been forgotten, each individual will want to get along by himself and be superior. One will abolish civil and ecclesiastical powers, all order and all justice will be trampled under foot; one will see nothing but homicides, hatred, jealousy, deceit, and discord, without love for one's country or for one's family.

15. The Holy Father will suffer greatly. I will be with him in the end in order to receive his sacrifice.

16. The wicked will make multiple attempts on his life without being able to harm him, but neither he, nor his successor... will see the Church of God triumph.

17. *Civil governments will all have the same design, which will be to abolish and make disappear all religious principle, to replace it with materialism, atheism, spirituality, and all sorts of vice.*

18. *In the year 1865, one will see an abomination in holy places; in convents, the flowers of the Church will be purified and the demon will present himself as the king of hearts. Would that those who are at the head of religious communities keep a close eye on the people they must admit, because the demon will use all his malice to introduce into religious orders people given to sin, for disorders and love of carnal pleasures will have spread throughout the earth.*

19. *France, Italy, Spain, and England will be at war; blood will flow through the streets; Frenchmen will fight against Frenchmen, Italians against Italians; then there will be a general war that will be terrifying. For a time, God will no longer remember France nor Italy, because the Gospel of Jesus Christ is no longer known. The wicked will deploy all their malice; people will kill each other, massacre each other even in their homes.*

20. *With the first blow of the violent sword, the mountains and the entire earth will tremble with terror, because the disorders and crimes of men pierce the vault of heaven. Paris will be burnt down and Marseille swallowed up; many large cities will be shaken and swal-*

lowed up by earthquakes: one will think that
everything is lost; one will see only homicides, one will hear only the sound of arms
and blasphemies. The just will suffer much;
their prayers, their penance, and their tears
will mount to Heaven, and all God's people
will ask for forgiveness and mercy, and will
ask for my aid and my intercession. Then Jesus Christ, by an act of justice and with his
great compassion for the just, will command
his angels such that all his enemies should be
struck dead. All of a sudden, the persecutors
of the Church of Jesus Christ and all men giv-
en to sin will perish, and the earth will become like a desert. Then peace will be had,
the reconciliation of God with men; Jesus
Christ will be served, adored, and glorified;
charity will flourish everywhere. The new
kings will be the right arm of the Holy
Church, which will be strong, humble, pious,
poor, zealous and imitative of the virtues of
Jesus Christ. The Church will be preached everywhere, and men will make great progress
in the faith, because there will be unity among
the workers of Jesus Christ, and men will live
in the fear of God.

21. That peace among men will not last long;
twenty-five years of abundant crops will make
them forget that men's sins are the cause of
all the troubles plaguing the earth.

22. A precursor of the Antichrist, with his troops
of many nations, will combat against the true

Christ, the only Savior of the world; he will spill a great quantity of blood and will wish to annihilate God's cult in order to make himself be seen like a God.

23. *The earth will be struck by all sorts of wounds (over and above the plague and famine which will be widespread); there will be wars until the last war, which will be waged then by the ten kings of the Antichrist, the which kings will have all the same goal, and they will be the only ones who govern the world. Before that happens, there will be a kind of false peace in the world; one will think of entertaining oneself; the wicked will give themselves over to all sorts of sin; but the children of the Holy Ghost, the children of the faith, my true imitators, will believe in the love of God and in the virtues that are dearest to me. Happy are the humble souls led by the Holy Ghost! I will fight with them until they arrive at the plenitude of the age.*

24. *Nature demands vengeance for men, and it shivers with fear in expectation of what must come to earth, which is soiled with crimes.*

25. *Tremble, earth, and you who profess to serve Jesus Christ and who, secretly, adore yourselves, tremble; for God will deliver you unto his enemy, because the holy places are in a state of corruption; many convents are no longer houses of God, but pasturages of Asmodeus and his lot.*

26. It will be during that time that the Antichrist will be born, of a Hebrew woman religious, of a false virgin who will have communication with the old serpent, the master of impurity; its father will be Ev.; while giving birth, it will vomit blasphemies, it will have teeth; in a word, it will be the devil incarnate; it will let out frightening cries, it will make prodigies, it will nourish itself on impurities. It will have brothers who, although not incarnate devils like it, will be children of evil; at 12 years old, they will make a name for themselves by their valiant victories; soon, they will each be at the head of their armies, assisted by the legions of hell.

27. The seasons will have changed, the earth will produce only bad fruit, the stars will lose their regular movements, the moon will reflect only a faint reddish glow; water and fire will cause convulsive movements and horrible earthquakes in the world, which will swallow up mountains and cities, (etc.)

28. Rome will lose its faith and become the seat of the Antichrist.

29. Demons of the air, with the Antichrist, will be great prodigies on earth and in the air, and men will be more and more perverted. God will take care of his faithful servants and men of goodwill; the Gospel will be preached everywhere, all people and all nations will have knowledge of the truth!

30. I address the present appeal to the earth; I appeal to the true disciples of God, living and reigning in heaven; I appeal to the true imitators of Christ made man, the only and true Savior of men; I appeal to my children, my true devotees, those who have given themselves to me in order that I might lead them to my divine Son, those whom I carry so to speak in my arms, those who have lived in my spirit; finally, I appeal to the Apostles of the last days, the faithful disciples of Jesus Christ who have lived in contempt of the world and of themselves, in poverty and humility, in contempt and in silence, in orison and in mortification, in chastity and in union with God, in suffering and ignorance of the world. It is time that they come out and enlighten the earth. Go and show yourselves as my cherished children; I am with you and in you, provided that your faith be the light that enlightens you in these days of misfortune. Would that your zeal make you as if famished for the glory and honor of Jesus Christ. Combat, children of light, you small number who see; for this is the time of times, the end of ends.

31. The Church will be eclipsed, the world will be in consternation. But witness Enoch and Eli filled with the Spirit of God; they will preach with the force of God, and men of goodwill will believe in God, and many souls will be consoled; they will make great progress by virtue of the Holy Ghost and will condemn the diabolical errors of the Antichrist.

32. *Woe unto the inhabitants of the earth! there will be bloody wars and famines; pestilences and contagious diseases; there will be rains of hail frightening to animals; thunders that shake entire cities; earthquakes that swallow up entire countries; one will hear voices in the air; men will beat their heads against walls; they will call on death, and, from another corner, death will be their torture; blood will flow from every side. Who will be able to vanquish, if God does not reduce the time of the ordeal? By the blood, tears, and the prayers of the just, God will allow himself to be swayed; Enoch and Eli will be put to death; pagan Rome will disappear; fire from Heaven will fall and consume three cities; all the universe will be struck with terror, and many will be seduced because they have not adored the true Christ living among them. It is time; the sun darkens; faith alone will survive.*

33. *Witness the times; the abyss will open wide. Witness the god of the gods of darkness. Witness the beast with his subjects, calling himself the savior of the world. He will rise up into the air with pride and go as far as heaven; he will be suffocated by the breath of the holy Archangel Michael. He will fall, and the earth, which, for three days, will be in a continual revolution, will open up its bosom full of fire; it will be plunged forever with its own into the eternal gulfs of hell. Then water and fire will purify the earth and consume all*

men's works of pride, and all will be re-
newed; and God will be served and glorified.

IV

Then the Holy Virgin gave me, also IN FRENCH, the
Rule for a new religious Order.

After having given me the Rule for that new
religious Order, the Holy Virgin took up again the
following Discourse:

"If they should be converted, the stones and
rocks will turn into wheat, and potatoes will be found
planted in the fields. Do you say your prayers, my
children?"

We both responded:

"Oh!, no, Madam, not much."

"Ah! my children, you must do it, morning
and evening, When you can do no better, say a Pater
and an Ave Maria*; and when you have time and*
when you can do better, you will say more.

"The only people who go to Mass are a few
old women; the others work all summer on Sunday;
and in winter, when they don't know what to do, they
go to Mass but only to mock religion. During Lent,
they go the butcher's shop like dogs.[126]

---

[126]Original footnote: the very pure Virgin makes use of an
energetic expression, to make it felt that, in a single example of
intemperance, she wants to tarnish the hideous wounds of
sensualism. Unable to reveal those wounds before the children,
she gives us a sign of it sufficiently: not only in the language of

"Have you not seen the ruined wheat, my children?"

Both of them gasped: "Oh! no, Madame."

The Holy Virgin addressing herself to Maximin: *"But you, my child, you must have seen it once near Coin, (?) with your father. The man in the room said to your father: 'Come see my wheat which is ruined.' You went. Your father took two or three spikes in his hand, he rubbed them together, and powder fell out of them. Then, when the both of you were no more than half an hour from Corps, your father turning to you gave you a morsel of bread and said: 'Here, my child, eat this year, for I don't know who will eat next year, if the wheat is ruined like that.'"*

Maximin responded: "That's true, Madame, I forgot."

The Very Holy Virgin ended her Discourse in French: *"Ah well! my children, you will pass it on to 'all my people.'"*

The Very Beautiful Lady crossed the rivulet; and, two paces away, without turning around to look at us, who were following her (because she attracted us to her by her brightness and even more so by her goodness, which intoxicated me, which seemed to me like it was melting my heart), she said again:

"Ah well! my children, you will pass it on to all 'my people.'"[127]

---

the Holy Scripture, but in all languages, the word "dogs" designates sinners who hid the shame of their vices.

Then she continued walking to the place where I had climbed up earlier in order to see where my animals had gotten off to. Her feet touched only the tips of the grass without bending them. Having arrived at the top of a small height, the Beautiful Lady stopped, and quickly I placed myself in front of her for to see, for to get a good look at her, and to try to know what path she was most inclined to take; for it was over for me, I had forgotten the animals and the masters whom I was working for; I had attached myself to *My* Lady, forever and without condition; yes, I never wanted, ever, to quit her side; I followed her without a second thought, and in the disposition to serve her as long as I lived.

With *My* Lady, I believed I had forgotten paradise; I no longer had any thought but to serve her in everything; and I believed I could do everything she would have told me to do, for it seemed to me that She had a great deal of power. She looked at me with a tender kindness which attracted me to her; I would have wanted, with my eyes closed, to throw myself

---

[127]Original footnote: The Holy Virgin shows the importance she attaches to her teaching. She came, in effect, to lead us back to the observation "*in spiritu et veritate*" of GOD's Law. She has so well summarized, in her discourse, the teachings of her Son, that it is impossible to speak in a useful manner to Christians, religious, and ecclesiastics of our time, without reverting, intentionally or not, to what she just said. Also, after having begun as her Son: "*pœnitemini*" (Mark 1:15). "*If my people do not wish to submit*," she terminates as he does, "*Docete omnes gentes*" (Math. 28:19). "You will pass it on to all my people." These last words, she repeats them. A sovereign never repeats an order he has just given; but She makes it understood to the children that, the first time, it had to do with that part of her discourse destined to be made public immediately, and the second time [it had to do with] the secrets.

into her arms. She did not give me the time to do so. She rose imperceptibly to a height of about one meter or more off the ground; and, remaining thus suspended in the air for a very short instant, My Beautiful Lady looked up at the Sky, then at the earth to her right and to her left, then She looked down at me with both her eyes, which were so gentle, so amiable and so good, that I believed she was drawing me inside her, and it seemed to me that my heart was opening up to hers.

And while my heart was melting in sweet dilatation, My Good Lady's beautiful face disappeared little by little: the moving light seemed to me to be multiplied or even condensed around the Very Holy Virgin so as to prevent me from seeing her any longer. Thus, the light replaced parts of her body so that she disappeared before my eyes; or it seemed that My Lady's body had changed into light while it melted away. Thus the light in the shape of a globe rose slowly in a direction to the right.[128]

I cannot say whether the volume of light diminished as she rose, or whether it was the distance

---

[128]Original footnote: Maximin: "We no longer saw anything but a globe of fire that rose and penetrated the firmament. – In our naïve language we called that globe a second sun. Our eyes were for a long time fixed on the place where the luminous globe had disappeared. I cannot depict for you here the ecstasy that we found ourselves in. I speak only for myself; I am quite aware that my entire being was wiped out, that each organic system had stopped in my person. When we had gotten a grip on ourselves, Mélanie and I, we looked at each other unable to say a single word, sometimes raising our eyes to heaven, other times at our feet and around us, other times still interrogating with our gaze everything that was around us. We seemed to be looking for the resplendent person whom I could no longer see."

that made it seem like the light was diminishing as she rose; what I do know is that I remained with my head raised and my eyes fixed on the light, even after that light, which continued to go off into the distance and grow smaller in volume, had finally disappeared.

My eyes look away from the firmament, I look around me, I see Maximin who looks at me, and I say to him: "Mémin, that must be the good God of my father,[129] or the Holy Virgin, or some great saint." And Maximin throwing his hands up into the air, he said, "Ah! if I had only known!"

---

[129]Original footnote: Here is a passage that has certainly seemed quite insignificant to a good number of readers. Mélanie who takes the Beautiful Lady for "the good GOD of my father"! What style! What a singular idea to write for us in this way, in the complete, official record of the Great Event, that childish, if not to say naughty, remark! Was that done to liven up the narration by Maximin's rather down-to-earth response, he who, usually, has more original repartees?... Really, that short line is quite insignificant...

For those who have had the good fortune of knowing the pious narrator personally, that anodyne line is one of the most charming in the story. It makes it come alive for them; it recalls to them one of the fine character traits of that individual who was as admirable in reality as she was avid to remain in the shadows and be forgotten.

"Mémin, that must be the good God of my father." Does that phrase appear merely insignificant to you – do you not also find it a bit *shocking*, if you remember the allusion we already made with respect to multiple celestial apparitions that Mélanie's childhood had favored her with? How is that possible! For a dozen years she lived in the nearly constant familiarity of Her whom she called her Mother; and, on September 19, [suddenly] she does not recognize her! She was so grossly mistaken! She took her for the "Good GOD of her father"! Who is mocking whom here? Is it not an effrontery rather than an "insignificant phrase"?...

V

On the evening of September 19, we returned a little later than usual. Having arrived at my masters' place, I busied myself with securing the animals and making sure everything was in order in the stable. I was not done when my mistress came to me as I was weeping and said: "Why, my child, did you not come to tell me what happened to you on the mountain?" (Maximin, not having found his masters, who had not returned yet from their labors, had come to mine and

---

And we who had the joy of seeing Mélanie up close, that phrase that she recalls to have spoken to Maximin fills us with joy! We see her, that day then, as we had always known her.

She is not mocking Maximin, of course, no more than she is mocking, for example, me towards the end of her life, by letting me believe that it was by inattention, indifference, laziness, or originality that she arrived late, or even did not arrive at all to church, at her usual hour, one or two days a week. I would have never gotten to the bottom of the mystery if, one day of similar absence, I had visited her unannounced, without giving her enough time to put away the material proof of her bloody stigmata. And, despite herself, pressed by my questions, she admitted to me that our crucified Lord, appearing to her, involved her in the sufferings of his Passion... And everything that one will learn about her, one day, is by similar means what one has learnt about her by chance...

Oh! how beautiful was the humility in that soul that the "Kind Brother" had formed! It was indeed Him who had instructed that soul, with the "*Sacramentum Regis*," the difficult art of "hiding the King's secret"! Those effusions of divine intimacies, she had to conceal them from every stranger's view... and one would say that all the work of her exterior life consisted in hiding them. A soul who is in a quasi uninterrupted relationship with the supernatural world and who must not let anyone notice it! A soul who is at the school of Him who is omniscient, and who must not know anything!... She had taken the proper means, she placed herself instinctively at the level of those with whom she spoke.

had recounted all that he had seen and heard.) I told her, "I wanted to tell you, of course, but I wanted to finish up my work first." A moment later, I went into the house, and my mistress said to me, "Tell me what you saw; the Shepherd of Bruite (that was the surname of Pierre Selme, Maximin's master) has told me everything."

I begin, and, towards the middle of the recitation, my masters come in from the fields; my mis-

---

I have given testimony, on this subject, of truly stupefying things and that perhaps, one day, the hour will come to tell it... On September 19, she was a child, and she spoke to Maximin as a child would have spoken. That is so natural that she did not notice even that she inserted the most beautiful of virtues into her work; and quite simply, beyond any doubt, she practices it, she is completely steeped in it, before the public eye: for when one publishes a recitation like hers, one really puts oneself in the middle of the crowd! But what difference does that make to her? She does not think about it! And she writes that "insignificant" phrase: "That must be the good GOD of my father"!...

On the evening of that great day, her mistress will find her in the stable IN TEARS. Those tears that she had held back in front of Maximin, she will know how to hold them back again, the moment she finds that she is not alone. She must not cry except in secret about those things that she must appear the unconscious messenger of, but which she has too well understood... Moreover, what difference does it make that she was or was not in tears? Nobody thinks to ask: Why? She cut short all curiosity with that childish phrase about "the good GOD of her Father."

I have expressed myself poorly just now, by saying that Mélanie put herself on the level of her milieu. Would anyone see in those words something of an arrogant condescension that compelled her, not without some disdain, in that direction? No, it is not she who put herself on that level. She had only to let herself go: it is the "Kind Brother" who did everything.

tress, who was weeping while listening to the laments and threats made by our tender Mother, said, "Ah! you need to go and harvest the wheat tomorrow; mark my words, and come hear what happened today to this child and Selme's Shepherd." And turning to me, she said, "Start from the beginning, everything you told me." I start over; and when I finished my Master said, "It's the Holy Virgin, or a great saint, who has come on the part of the good God; but it's as if the good God had come himself; one must do everything that Saint said. How do you plan to tell it to all her people?" I told him this, "You tell me how I must do it, and I will do it." Then, he added while looking at his own mother, his wife, and his brother, "We need to think." Then each went about his business.

It was after supper. Maximin and his masters came to mine to recount what Maximin had told them, and to understand what needed to be done. "For," they said, "it seems to us that it is the Holy Virgin who was sent by the good God; the words that She said make one believe it. And She told them to pass it on to all her people; it may be these two chil-dren need to travel around the world to make it known that everyone must observe the command-ments of the good God, otherwise great misfortune will happen to us." After a moment of silence, my master said, while addressing Maximin and myself,

---

In his hands, the humble soul has merely to be ready: Mélanie quite simply readied herself. And that was really so simple that no one thought to be surprised by it. Our Lord makes souls like that who are only for Him, beautiful flowers for his "Closed Garden." The Shepherdess disappeared rather well in that long recitation wherein, however, she was perpetually on stage!...

"You know what you need to do, my children? To-morrow, get up early, go the both of you to Monsieur the Curate, and tell him everything you saw and heard; tell him exactly how it came to pass; he will tell you what you need to do."

On September 20, the day after the apparition, I left early with Maximin. Arrived at the Curate's, I

The hour will come, which I wait for impatiently, to lift all the veils, "*Opera Dei revelare honorificum est*." Would that it might suffice us, for the moment, to admire all those divine precautions without trying to understand them. Our Lord loved that soul so much that he wanted her for Himself and nothing but for Himself. And she, how she submitted, docile and simple, to all her celestial Friend's exigencies! Take her[, for example,] two years after the Apparition: the writers have too soon said to us that up until the age of 17 and despite the efforts of the women Religious of Corps, she was unable to have been sufficiently instructed to receive her first communion and could not understand the alphabet. (In order for her to read, they did not teach her out loud the *letter* of the catechism: "When you know how to read, they said to her, you will understand it in your book and you will take your first communion.") They take that as the facile occasion for a clever commentary on the text: "*Quæ stulta sunt mundi elegit Deus ut confundat sapientes*." It is hard however for a young girl to pass for a dolt at this point! To receive lessons from the great doctor, from Eternal Wisdom in person, to have been educated in that school and to be unable before the jury of the first communion to recite the *letter* of the catechism!... Didn't anyone notice, all of a sudden, without her realizing it herself, that she was as instructed as all her classmates... Her 17 years will explain everything: it is entirely natural of course that a young girl, 17 years of age, profoundly ignorant the day before, should know how to read from one day to the next. Nobody was surprised by that; and one could see finally that child, for so long limited in intelligence, take her place among the ranks of the little communicants of eleven years old. The entire parish of Corps was convinced that she was taking communion for the first time... How well the "Kind Brother" hid her secrets! No, the "Little Sister" did not put herself on its level; it was He who put her, for love, well below that level as a "preventative measure."

knocked on the door. Monsieur the Curate's domestic came to open up and asked what we wanted. I told her (in French, me who had never spoken it before): "We would like to speak with Monsieur the Curate."

"And what do you wish to tell him?" she asked us.

"We wish to tell him, Mademoiselle, that yesterday we were watching our animals on the mountain of Baisses, and after having eaten, etc., etc." We told her a good deal of the Very Holy Virgin's discourse. Then the church bell rang; it was the last call for Mass. Monsieur the Abbot Perrin, curate of La Salette, who had overheard us, opened the door loudly; he was crying; he was beating his chest; he said to us, "My children, we are doomed, the good God is going to punish us. Ah! my God, it's the Holy Virgin who has appeared to you!" And he left to say the Holy Mass. We looked at each other, Maximin, the domestic, and I; then Maximin said to me, "I'm gong home to my dad, in Corps." And we separated.

Not having received an order from my Masters to return immediately after having spoken with Monsieur the Curate, I thought there would be no harm in my attending Mass. I was in Church then. The Mass began, and, after the first Gospel reading, Monsieur the Curate turns to the people and tries to tell his parishioners about the apparition that had just taken place, the evening before, on one of their Mountains, and exhorts them no longer to work on Sunday; his voice was broken up by sobs, and everyone was moved. After Holy Mass, I returned to my masters' place. Monsieur Peytard, who is the Mayor of La Salette (even then), came to interrogate me on the event of the apparition; and, after having satisfied himself as to the truth of what I was saying, retired convinced.

I continued to remain in the service of my Masters until the Feast of All Saints. Then I was placed as a boarder among the women religious of Providence, in my region, at Corps.

VI

The Very Holy Virgin was very tall and well proportioned; she appeared so light that a breeze could have moved her, even though she was immobile and well poised. Her physiognomy was majestic, imposing, but not in the way Lords here below are imposing. She instilled a deferential fear. At the same time as Her Majesty instilled respect combined with love, she drew one to Her. Her gaze was gentle and penetrating; her eyes seemed to speak to mine, but the conversation came from a deep and vibrant feeling of love; her ravishing beauty made me melt. The sweetness of her gaze, her attitude of incomprehensible kindness, made me understand and feel what it was that drew me to Her and what made me want to give myself to her; it was an expression of love that cannot be expressed in the language of the flesh or with the letters of the alphabet.

The clothing that the Very Holy Virgin wore was silvery white and brilliant; there was *nothing material* about it; it was composed of light and glory, varying and scintillating. On earth, there is no expression for it or any comparison to give.

The Holy Virgin was completely beautiful and made entirely of love; on looking at her I was languishing to melt and blend with her. Around her, as in her person, everything respired of the majesty, splendor, and magnificence of an incomparable Queen. She appeared beautiful, white, immaculate, crystalized, dazzling, celestial, fresh, new like a Virgin; the word *Love* seemed to escape from her argentine lips and every pore. She appeared to me like a good Mother, full of kindness, amiability, love for us, compassion, mercy.

The crown of roses she wore on her head was so gorgeous, so brilliant, it was unimaginable; the roses, of various colors, were not of this earth; it was a bouquet of flowers that encircled the head of the Very Holy Virgin in the shape of a crown; but the roses changed or were replaced; then, from the center of each rose was emitted so beautiful a light that it ravished the roses and gave them a blinding beauty. From the crown of roses something like branches of gold and a quantity of other small flowers, mixed together with diamonds, rose up.

Altogether it made for a very beautiful diadem, that shone all by itself, brighter than the earth's sun.

The Holy Virgin had a very pretty Cross suspended from her neck. That Cross appeared to be made of gold; I say gold so as not to say gold-plated; for I have sometimes seen golden objects of various nuances of gold, which made, in my eyes, a very beautiful effect compared to simple gold-plating. On her most beautiful Cross, all brilliant with light, was a Christ, was Our Lord, his arms extended on the Cross. Almost to either end of the Cross, on one side of which was a hammer, and on the other a pincers. The Christ had the color of natural flesh, but he shined with a great brilliance; and the light that was emitted from his entire body appeared like very brilliant darts, which cleaved the heart with the desire to melt in him. Sometimes the Christ appeared to be dead; his head hung to a side, and his body sagged, as if he was about to fall, if he hadn't been held up by the nails that kept him fixed on the Cross.

I had a vivid compassion for him, and I would have wanted to retell his unknown love to the entire world, and to infiltrate in mortal souls the most heart-felt love and keenest recognition towards a God who had no need for us to be what he is, what he was, and what he will forever be; and however, O incomprehensible love for man! he made himself man, and he wanted to die, yes to die, to better engrave in our souls and in our memory the Mad love that he has for us! Oh! how miserable I am to find myself so poor in expression to retell the love, yes, the love of our good Savior for us! but on the other hand, how fortunate we are to be able to feel more than what we cannot express!

At other times, the Christ seemed alive; he held his head straight, kept his eyes open, and he appeared to be on the Cross of his own volition. Sometimes also he appeared to speak: he seemed to want to show that he was on the Cross for us, out of love for us, so as to attract us to his love, that he always has new love for us, that his love from the beginning and from the year 33 is always that of today and will be forever.

The Holy Virgin was weeping nearly the entire time that She spoke to me. Her tears dropped one by one slowly down to her knees; then, as if with a sparkling of light, she disappeared. She was brilliant, blinding, and full of love. I would have wanted to console Her, and that She might stop weeping. But She seemed to need to show her tears to better show her love, forgotten by men. I would have wanted to rush into her arms and tell her: "My good Mother, do not cry! I want to love you for everyone on earth." But She seemed to say to me: "There are so many who do not know me!"

I was vacillating between life and death, while seeing so much love on the one hand, so much desire to be loved, and on the other hand so much coldness, so much indifference... Oh! my Mother, all Mother, completely beautiful and completely lovable, my love, heart of my heart!...

The tears of our tender Mother, far from diminishing her majestic appearance as a Queen and as a Mistress, seemed, on the contrary, to embellish her, to make her more lovely, more beautiful, more powerful, more filled with love, more maternal, more ravishing; and I would have eaten those tears, that made my heart leap with compassion and love. To see a Mother weeping, and such a Mother, without making all imaginable efforts to console her, to turn her sorrow to joy, is that even comprehensible? O Mother,

better than good! You were fashioned of all preroga-
tives that God is capable of; you have as if exhausted
God's power; you are good, and then good in the
goodness of God even; God has grown greater by
making you his earthly and heavenly work of art.

The Very Holy Virgin had a yellow apron on.
What am I saying, yellow? She wore an apron that
was brighter than many suns put together. It was not
of a material fabric, it was composed of glory, and
that glory was scintillating and of a ravishing beauty.
Everything in the Very Holy Virgin carried me along
strongly, and made me as if to smoothly slide into a
love and adoration of my Jesus, in all states and conditions of his mortal life.

The Very Holy Virgin had two chains, one a
little larger than the other. From the narrower one was
suspended the Cross that I mentioned earlier. Those
chains (as that is how they need to be described) were
like the rays of glory issuing from a great, varying,
and scintillating spark.

Her shoes (as that is the only word for it)[130]
were white, but of a silvery whiteness, shiny; there
were roses around them. Those roses were of a dazzling beauty, and from the center of each rose issued
a very beautiful flame of light, very agreeable to look
on. On her shoes, there was a golden buckle, not of
the gold of the earth, but of the gold of paradise.

---

[130]Original footnote: "When I have to speak of the Beautiful Lady
who appeared to me on the Holy Mountain, I feel the
embarrassment that Saint Paul must have felt coming down from
the third heaven. No, the eye of man has never seen, his ear has
never heard, what was given to me to see and to hear.

The sight of the Very Holy Virgin was itself an actual paradise. She had in Herself all that could satisfy, for the earth was forgotten.

The Holy Virgin was surrounded by two lights. The first light, closer to the Very Holy Virgin, came towards us; it shone with a very beautiful brightness and scintillated. The second light extended a little more around the Beautiful Lady, and we found ourselves contained in it; it was motionless (that is to say it did not scintillate), but was much brighter than

---

"How would ignorant children, called to explain themselves on such extraordinary things, how would they have met a justness of expression that elite minds do not always find to depict vulgar objects. One should not be surprised then if what we have called *bonnet, crown, scarf, chains, roses, apron, gown, socks, buckles,* and *shoes* had hardly those same forms. In that beautiful costume, there was nothing terrestrial; the rays alone, of different nuances, blended with each other, produced a collective magnificence that we have diminished and materialized.

"An expression has no other value than to give the idea that one attaches to it; but where to find, in our language, expressions to render things that men have no idea about. There was a light, but a light very different from all others; it went directly to my heart without passing through my organs but with a harmony however that the most beautiful concerts would be unable to reproduce, – What am I saying? With a savorousness that the most sweet liquors are not known to possess.

"I do not know what comparisons to employ because comparisons taken from the sensible world are affected by the failing that I reproach the words of our language with; they do not offer to the mind any idea of what I wish to give. When at the end of a firework display a crowd shouts out: "There's the bouquet," – is there a very close relationship between a collection of flowers and an ensemble of rockets that explode? No, assuredly not; eh, well! the distance that separates the comparisons that I employ and the ideas that I want to give is even more considerable, infinitely."

our earth's poor sun. All those lights did not harm our eyes and did not tire our view.

In addition to those lights, all that splendor, there issued even more groups or fasces of light, or rays of light, from the Body of the Holy Virgin, and from her clothes and from everywhere.

The Beautiful Lady's voice was sweet; it enchanted, ravished, made one's heart feel good; it appeased, removed all obstacles, calmed, softened. It seemed to me that I would have wished to feast on her beautiful voice forever, and my heart seemed to dance or want to go meet it and melt in it.

The eyes of the Very Holy Virgin, our tender Mother, cannot be described by human language. To speak of them, one would need be a seraph. One would also need, one would need the language of God himself, of that God who created the Immaculate Virgin, a work of art of his almightiness.

The eyes of the August Mary appeared thousands of times more beautiful than brilliants, diamonds, and the most sought-after precious stones; they shined like two suns; they were gentle like gentleness itself, clear like mirrors. In her eyes one saw paradise; they attracted you to Her; it seemed that She wanted to give herself and entice. The more I looked at her, the more I wanted to see her; the more I saw, the more I loved her, and I loved her with all my strength.

The eyes of the Immaculate Beauty were like God's gate, through which one saw all that could intoxicate the soul. When the Mother of God's eyes met with mine, I felt inside myself a happy revolution of love and protestation, to love her and to melt with her in love.

While looking at each other, our eyes spoke each in their own way, and I loved her so much that I would have wanted to embrace her in the middle of her eyes which softened my soul and seemed to entice it and make it blend with hers. Her eyes planted a sweet sensation of trembling throughout my entire being; and I was afraid to make the least movement, however small, that might be disagreeable to her.

That single look in the eyes of the purest of Virgins would have sufficed as Heaven for a blessed man; would have sufficed, among all the events that happened over the course of a mortal man's life, to make a soul enter into the Almighty's plenitude of wills; would have sufficed to make that soul offer continual acts of praise, thanks, reparation, and expiation. That single look concentrates the soul in God and renders it as if dead-alive, making all things on earth, even things that seem the most serious, appear like a child's playthings; it would have wanted to hear speak only of God and of what touches on his Glory.

Sin is the only evil that She sees on earth. She would die of sorrow because of it, if God did not sustain her. Amen.[131]

– Mary of the Cross, Victim of Jesus, born Mélanie Calvat, Shepherdess of La Salette. Castel-

---

[131]Original footnote: "Amen, God's will be done!" Immense suffering and continual abandonment to the divine will... How the holy child admirably depicts herself in that impersonal cry which is here of such sublime simplicity!

lammare, November 21, 1878.

Nihil obstat: imprimatur.

Datum Lycii ex Curia Ep., die 15 Nov. 1879.

Vicarius Generalis

CARMELUS ARCH^us COSMA.

The knowledge that GOD gave her of the sins committed here on earth, the "smell" of sin being the *only* suffering that she complained of... To expiate, she wept so much that she went blind during her stay in Darlington. She recovered her sight by a miracle, but her tears having never stopped flowing, her sight became very weak.

Appendix 3: Funeral Oration

FUNERAL ORATION
of
Sister MARY of the CROSS,
née Mélanie CALVAT

Shepherdess of La Salette

Given in Messina and, at the anniversary Service,
in the Cathedral of Altamura,
by the Canon Annibal-Marie of France.
Published with the Imprimatur by Monseigneur Letterio,
Archbishop of Messina.

> "*Cantabiles mihi erant justificationes tuæ
> in loco peregrinationis meæ.*"

> "*J'ai chanté vos justifications dans le lieu
> de mon pèlinerage.*" (Ps. 118:54)[132]

An angelic creature, a pure ideal of innocence and virtue, a human being without blemish, very sweet, full of the holiest aspirations for God, his glory, and his eternal Love – has passed through this valley of tears.

When a person loved by us departs, there re-

---

[132]*Cantabiles... pèlerinage*: Latin, and then French, for "Thy justifications were the subject of my song, in the place of my pilgrimage." Psalms 118:54.

mains an emptiness that one would like to fill with the remembrance of their dear person and with the tears shed over the grave that contains the beloved's remains. Religion sanctifies that feeling and raises it to the sublime. It convokes us at funeral ceremonies, puts prayers and canticles on our lips, makes us participate in the Great Sacrifice of Expiation, and writes on the tomb of those who are no longer: *Qui credit in me, etiam si mortuus fuerit, vivet.*[133]

But when the exceptional case presents itself that the departed was one of those rare souls, consecrated to the highest perfections, in which is found I do not know what supernatural and divine characteristic, when its affections are held not only within the bounds of nature, but have presented the imprint of eternal Charity, when the phases of their life and death are accompanied by events and circumstances that are out of the ordinary, oh! then the tomb of that elect creature is an altar, their memory a benediction, the funeral ceremonies themselves, the plaintive notes of the organ, and the lugubrious voices of the cantors, change into a festive hymn, or even form the echo of celestial canticles whose angels accompany that soul in the accomplishment of its pilgrimage to the kingdom of Glory.

And such are the solemn obsequies and ceremonies whose tribute we offer today to our beloved departed, to MÉLANIE CALVAT, the famous shepherdess of La Salette.

Feelings of affection and faith, intimate grati-

---

[133]*Qui... vivet*: Latin for "And whosoever liveth and believeth in me shall never die." John 11:26.

tude, and a saintly veneration, those are the emotions that we feel, reminding us of her before God and men. She belonged to us: it was a great love that she had for us, great also was the love we had for her. Now we search for a comfort for our suffering, we want to place ourselves in relationship with that dear, beautiful, innocent soul, totally impregnated with the love of JESUS and MARY, which, nevertheless, palpitates for us; we want to invoke her on earth, so that she might hear us in Heaven; we want to ask for her mediation, that she might pray for us.

You, young sisters who, together with your orphans, had her for more than a year as your Mother and your Mistress of sublime virtue, you feel the exceptionally keen need to testify to that holy soul, one more time, how great your feelings of veneration, tenderness, and love are for her.

So have courage, then, let us contemplate her in Faith, bright and smiling, even though invisible to us in that holy temple (*innixa dilecto suo*), leaning on her Beloved, and let us begin her praise after having invoked the name of JESUS.

MÉLANIE of La Salette was born in Corps, small burg of France, in the diocese of Grenoble, on November 7, 1831, of respectable parents. Her father was a mason and pit sawyer, and he was named PIERRE CALVAT. Her mother was named JULIE BARNAUD.

Historians of the celebrated apparition of the Very Holy Virgin at La Salette say that, before the great event, MÉLANIE was merely a poor little shep-

herdess, uncultivated and ignorant, incapable of understanding *Our Father*. But how wrong they are!
Great mysteries unfolded between GOD and her soul,
since childhood. Her good father, when she was only
three years old, showed her a Crucifix and said to her:
"See, my girl, how Our Lord Jesus Christ wanted to
die on the Cross out of love for us!" The small girl
fixed her attention and, as if lit up by a superior light,
seemed to have penetrated the intimate meaning of
those words and that image, in silence. Since then, an
interior impulsion pushed her to a love of the Cross
and of the Crucified. With an intelligence incompara-
bly beyond her years, She said: "The Crucifix of my
father does not speak, but it prays in silence, I want to
imitate it, I will keep quiet and I will pray in silence."
It was in that way that she prepared herself in contemplation. The young girl's mother, not a bad woman,
but irate, scolded her incessantly and ordered her to
leave the house. Little MÉLANIE smiled however and
forced herself to embrace that upset mother. One day,
she was nearly five years old, her mother ordered her
to leave and not come back. The poor little girl withdrew to a neighboring copse and lamented her sad
fate, as she wrote in one of her memoirs; she sat down
at the foot of a tree, tired and oppressed, and fell
asleep. A mysterious dream came to her and was like
a prelude to her entire life, to her entire earthly pilgrimage. In it she seemed to see the baby JESUS, same
age as herself, dressed in a rose-colored frock, who,
coming up to her, said to her: "Little sister, my dear
little sister, where are we going?" Inspired by divine
instinct, she replied, "To Calvary." Then, the celestial
child took her by the hand and led her to the holy

mountain. During that trip, the sky was covered with clouds and grew dark, and a great rain of crosses of all sizes fell on their shoulders. A crowd of people addressed her with insults and testified their contempt for her. Frightened, she squeezed the hand of her celestial guide, whose agreeable face she had lost sight of amidst the darkness. All of a sudden, she let go of the hand of her guide, and she fell into a deep desolation. Nonetheless, the trip ended and she arrived on Calvary. There, a horrible scene took place. From below, a gulf of fire opened up, into which multitudes of people threw themselves; with a frightened soul, and obeying a divine impulse, she offered herself as the victim of all suffering and the eternal salvation of souls, for the conversion of sinners.

At that moment, the small girl woke up; the sun was appearing on the horizon, that dream had lasted all night.

On return to her paternal home, she said nothing of what had happened to her the night before, but kept quiet in order to imitate her father's Crucifix. A new life of suffering and meditation began for her. The celestial child whom she had seen in a dream was always with her in her thoughts, she spoke to him in the innermost secrecy of her heart, she offered him her works and her sufferings, and it seemed to her that he always called her by that sweet name of "little sister, my dear little sister," to the point that whenever anyone asked her what her name was, she replied simply, "Little sister."

Thus hidden and absorbed by the precocious contemplations of a life filled with the immense

graces of heaven (*the revelation of which will doubtless cause a great surprise in the religious world*),
that creature of election, from an early age, drank in
silence from the chalice of humiliations and contempt, inhumanely chased multiple times from the
maternal home, and sent here and there in the service
of various peasant families.

One day, her irate mother wanting to be done
with her in some way, put her, as a punishment (She
told us herself, several years ago, smiling), in the service of a poor family of peasants who entrusted to her
the care of leading their animals to pasture on some
alpine mountains of La Salette.

Those mountains belong to the great chain of
French Alps, at an elevation of nearly 2000 meters
above sea level. There, winter is very harsh, but when
the sun rays shine on it it, on a beautiful day in spring
or summer, they offer a sublime and enchanting spectacle. In the distance, on high, at the horizon, a belt of
steep mountains, here some deep valleys and there, all
around, hills and plateaus covered in a green carpet of
mixed herbs and small wild flowers. That solitary
place, where one almost never saw a human being,
quickly became the delight of that innocent soul, hidden, separated from the world, and intimately united
with her Creator as it were. It was then that she tasted
the words of the learned doctor of Clairvaux:[134] "O
blessed solitude, O solitary blessedness!"

But what were the mysteries of divine love
that unfolded in those solitary places between that

---

[134]Learned doctor of Clairvaux: St. Bernard (1190-1153 AD), a
Burgundian abbot.

chosen soul and her God? It has been said: "I will lead you into solitude, and I will speak to your heart." She took pleasure, while her animals grazed, in speaking with the small flowers of the good GOD, as she called him, in inviting them to praise the Creator, and in pitying them for being unable to love him.

On September 19, 1846, a Saturday, on the mountain of La Salette, that celebrated apparition of the Very Holy Virgin appeared to the fortunate shepherdess and little MAXIMIN who, for one week, had been coming, him also, to that mountain with his animals.

The Holy Mother of GOD appeared with the signs of the Passion, weeping the whole time as she spoke to the two shepherds, menaced divine punishments because of contempt for and profanation of Sunday, and confided two secrets, one to MÉLANIE and the other to MAXIMIN. Before vanishing, the Holy Virgin had said: "MY LITTLE CHILDREN, ALL THAT I HAVE JUST CONFIDED IN YOU, MAKE IT KNOWN TO ALL MY PEOPLE."

That order by the Very Holy Virgin was the point of departure of another kind of life for the young shepherdess. She was as if yanked out of her dear solitude, lifted out of the oblivion and mystery of her hidden life, and invested with a mission that was bound to cause her suffering and tears, ovations and contempt, veneration and calumny, long peregrinations from country to country. "*Cantabiles mihi erant justificationes tuæ in loco peregrinationis meæ.*"[135]

It was only by the grace of a continual supernatural assistance that she could resist and persevere to the end.

The apparition of La Salette was a manifestation of the Mother of Sorrows. The Very Holy Virgin had appeared during the vespers that preceded the feast day of Our Lady of Seven Sorrows. She had a crucifix on her chest, as well as the hammer and pincers, eloquent symbol of the crushed and desolated mother.

From that moment on, MÉLANIE was called on to participate more intimately in the sorrows of JESUS and MARY.

Chased from France by Napoleon III, she went to England and practiced her profession among the Carmelites of Darlington.

When the moment came to publish the secret of La Salette, she was relieved of her vows by Pius IX and, since that day, who could speak to the multiple vicissitudes traversed by that unique creature?

Still young, at twenty-six years of age, she finds herself alone in the world, fugitive, wandering adventurously, a little bit in one country, a little bit in another. But her spirit as well as her heart found themselves always concentrated on a single point: the fulfillment of divine will. To whatever place she brought herself, it seemed that the atmosphere around her became purified and, by her attitude, everyone

---

[135]*Cantabilies... meæ*: Psalms 118:54.

was struck by her modesty, her suavity, and even her silence. When she found herself in Church, her meditation and her humble attitude gave a glimpse into her hidden sanctity. She was a stranger wherever she went, but when, after a certain time, she was recognized and became the subject of veneration, the pure dove of the Lord took flight for other regions.

In religion, she had taken the name of Sister Mary of the Cross, and she kept it. God wanted her incessantly crucified.

Gifted with an exquisite sensibility, with a sagacious and penetrating mind, profound and close in her affections, very sensitive in her compassion for human misery, very generous in her Zeal for divine glory and for the salvation of souls, she passed her entire life in a spiritual agony that can never be understood except in GOD. Her days and her nights were filled with incessant tears and with her moanings of a mystical dove. The lament of the Very Holy Virgin on the mountain of La Salette was always present in her mind, and she associated with it her tears which, in the end, went so far as to lower her gaze. But the lively and penetrating rays of her dark eyes, full of intelligence and contemplative, were not diminished.

It is at the school of suffering that the strong and robust temperings of the mind are fashioned. But what a difference between the heroes of religion and those of the century! The suffering of Saints is in the imitation of JESUS CHRIST, the pure love of GOD, love of the Cross, the triumph of grace over human weakness; it is a suffering that rejoices in giving proof of its love to the Loved One, which is drunk on suffering itself and makes it take part in that Mysterious thirst that makes the Divine Redeemer on the mountain of Sacrifice cry out: "*Sitio*," I am thirsty!

The suffering of souls who love GOD has very elevated motives and sublime ends. The heart, the soul, the senses, are placed as if in a crucible because GOD is not loved, because one is afraid to offend him, or often because, in the secrecy of the mind, the living Sun of Divine Presence finds itself obscured, or simply because the affectionate soul would like as if to be annihilated so that God might be glorified, or because it would want to leave the body and fly towards divine caresses, but that the hour and minute have not arrived. It is what makes the Prophet cry out: Alas, my pilgrimage has not been hard enough yet!

Such was the suffering of that privileged creature. Whatever her interior tribulations were, of a more than ordinary kind, this is not the place to depict them. She confessed to a person that, very young still, she had ten years of hell in her spirit. So people thought she was crazy or hallucinating, they led her to the Grande Chartreuse. Nonetheless, marvelous thing that one encounters only in the life of Saints, she herself had never grown tired of suffering for JESUS CHRIST. In her transports, she said: "I ask the Lord to make me suffer and to hide me." Veritable character of solid virtue and profound humility.

And now, I must not pass in silence over a long and holy martyrdom that that privileged saint suffered all her life.

Admitting even, with a purely human faith,

the apparition of the Very Holy Virgin of La Salette, we can equally admit, by virtue of diverse explicit declarations made by MÉLANIE CALVAT, that the Very Holy Virgin, from the moment she had confided a secret to her, had then revealed to her a remarkable religious order that would issue from the Holy Church, called the new Apostles or Missionaries of the Mother of GOD, which will expand throughout the world and do immense good for Catholicism. That congregation will consist of a second order and a Third Order. They will be impassioned for the glory of GOD and the salvation of souls, with an ardor similar to that of the first Apostles. The statements contained in MÉLANIE'S Secret, and through which the Very Holy Virgin announced the formation of that great religious order, possess nothing, in fact, of our humanity; they breathe a divine breath, they are simplicity put in harmony with the sublime. The Very Holy Virgin, after having announced that future event, gave to MÉLANIE the rule that that new religious order was to follow. MÉLANIE held that rule in her memory for twelve years, without having written it down. "It seemed imprinted in me," she said. Later, the moment designated by the Very Holy Virgin for divulgation of the Secret having arrived, MÉLANIE wrote down that rule, but then it became impossible for her to keep it present in her memory.

That rule was submitted to the judgment of a commission of cardinals of the Holy Church and judged by them irreproachable. It is like a chapter from the Gospel and contains the quintessence of Christian perfection put into practice with the greatest gentleness and charity.

Now MÉLANIE suffered a spiritual agony throughout her life, in the expectation of seeing the accomplishment of the Very Holy Virgin's word and the organization of the Holy Church's new Apostles. Far from it, she was witness to the persecutions that devotion to Our Lady of La Salette had to endure, by God's will, and to the point that with each persecution, that devotion seemed like it had to be dashed. Her gaze was always turned towards Rome, waiting for the supreme authority of the Church to crown La Salette with glory and honor, and that the foundation she sighed for should come to fruition finally. But the Holy See's prudence in like affair and divine Providence which rules over and disposes everything had brought that holy creature to a continual and perfect resignation of divine will. So, she will have said with Ezekias: *"Ecce in pace amaritudo mea amarissima!"*[136] Often she considered herself an obstacle to the accomplishment of the divine plan, and then she utterly effaced herself before God, mortified herself by various means and wished for death, sighed after it, asked for it in her prayers.

It is in that manner that that poor person who was exiled on earth chanted the canticle of her destinies. *"Cantabiles mihi erant justificationes tuæ in loco peregrinationis meæ."*

If what appeared on the mountain of La Salette was the Very Holy Virgin MARY, the immaculate Mother of GOD; if that was that incomparable Mary who confided her secret to MÉLANIE and to MAXIMIN, and gave a very sacred rule for a new, large

---

[136]*Ecce... amarissima*: Isaiah 38:17.

religious order of the last Apostles, who can doubt that the Queen of Heaven's promise must achieve its entire fulfillment? In that case, rejoice, O innocent shepherdess of La Salette, rejoice in GOD, O soul chosen from among a thousand; your long martyrdom has been merely a preparation for an extremely ineffable grace! The sacrifice of your simple life, offered in holocaust through sufferings and mortifications of all sorts, will be blessed by Jesus and Mary, and its fruit will be a generation of elect. And who will be able to name them? *Generationes ejus, quis enarrabit?*

How admirable GOD is in his works! MÉLANIE's humble, hidden, penitent life will have become, in the face of GOD's infinite goodness, a title to his compassion in favor of humanity; MÉLANIE's life, which began to be known and admired, now that she herself was separated from this world, will be perhaps a motive for hastening that divine rule, dictated by the Very Holy Virgin and, by consequence, the immense benefits that will ensue from it.

GOD knows the path of hearts. It is written that beautiful are the ways of Wisdom: "*Viæ ejus viæ pulchræ.*" When in the life of a holy creature, when a solid virtue is found joined to a collection of diverse situations, events, and intrinsic and extrinsic fruits, in which beauty, the sublime and the pathetic strike, entice, and invade the heart and imagination, – then all men are conquered and have gained the truth.

I thought I discovered something similar in that life and in the diverse peripeteia traversed by that elect of the Lord, to the point of not knowing if there was, in our epoch, in the world, another person who could be compared to her. The several memoirs that she wrote about herself, in obedience, will exceed those marvels. To begin with, it is a little girl who inhabits the woods, often surrounded by wild animals and divers birds, playing with one and the other; then it is a young, solitary shepherdess who conducts the sheep and cows into steep and savage places and there, seated in the shadow of a thick tree, prays or speaks with the flowers.

But see how the great splendors of the supernatural surround her, transport her as far as heaven. The All Beautiful, She who is light, love, grace, poetry of the Infinite, the Virgin Mary shows herself to Her, speaks to her. See how the name of the little, unknown shepherdess flies from mouth to mouth and fills the world.

Oh! how many have envied her fate! How many have desired to see her! to venerate her! how many have tried to kiss at least the hem of her clothing. But see her become more beautiful still from the continual effort and filled with the humility she took to hide herself! The fortunate shepherdess soon becomes a holy virgin, devoted to the Celestial Spouse.

The habits of penance, the silence of cloistered saints give a new shine to that celestial beauty. She was then in the flower of her twenty years.

A few years later, the shepherdess of La Salette, the inhabitant of the woods, the virginal dove finds herself devoted to the pilgrimage of the world, she enters into a new phase of her existence that will last all her life. For fifty years nearly, Mélanie of La

Salette fulfilled a mission or a sacrifice to which God destined her by his impenetrable ends. A nomadic life, wandering, from country to country, always in the hope of finding a place where she might hide herself from everyone, and where men would not offend GOD! "Some people," she said one day, "believe that I like traveling and going from place to place! but how mistaken they are!" And what motivations she had to justify her peregrinations!

But our city of Messina and this pious religious Institute of charity owe the sweet, gentle memory of the Lord's chosen saint to a stop she made on her diverse pilgrimages. It is quite right that we should evoke her saintly memory and that we should speak with you about it for a little while, as it is for Her that we are gathered here at the foot of the Holy Altar and that we celebrate this funeral ceremony.

Messina, the very holy Mary's city, received from time immemorial particular marks of love by Her who promised it her perpetual protection. It was seven years ago that MÉLANIE of La Salette came to reside here, for one year and 18 days. Her arrival was preceded by several signs that are held to be miraculous.

What gave birth to so great a good was that our Institute was then going through a period of difficulties such that it seemed to need to be suppressed. For some time, a sojourn of several hours at Castellammare di Stabia had reminded me of something I knew by hearsay, that is that the Shepherdess of La Salette was living there! Great was my desire to meet her, but that was in vain; because that fugitive dove had moved her nest elsewhere. She was living in Galatina, diocese of Lecce. I was left with an emptiness at heart.

On my return to Messina, I wrote to Mgr. Zola, of fortunate memory, then Bishop of Lecce, who graciously gave me Mélanie's address, and I soon entered into correspondence with the Lord's servant. Oh! what perfume of Sanctity her letters seemed to emit. I found myself transported into Paradise! One day she wrote to me that she was going to leave Galatina, but that she would not let anyone know her new address. That surprised me, and I decided to go find her to invite her to come to our Institute in Messina. It was for me like a trip of devotion to the Holy Virgin; I smiled at the thought of seeing and listening to that fortunate creature who had seen the Holy Mother of GOD and had heard her speak.

I saw Mélanie in her poor abode, I conversed with her, I heard her recount to me the Great Apparition of La Salette; and holy and deep were my emotions. I invited her to come to Messina, but she was undecided. She spoke to me with an affection for Messina, told me that she carried with her, printed, the Very Holy Virgin's letter to the inhabitants of Messina,[137] and showed me a translation of it in French. But in the end, she remained undecided. On return, I found my poor Institute near the brink of failure. Then I emboldened myself to expose our situation to the Elect of the Lord and renewed my invita-

---

[137]Original footnote: the city of Messina took great pride in possessing a letter that the Holy Virgin had written to its inhabitants who had just received the Christian faith.

tion to her, asking her to come at least for one year. Immediately, she responded to me that she had accepted, and that she would come with the purpose of organizing and forming that Community of Young Women of the Divine Zeal of the Heart of JESUS, who are dedicated to the education of orphans, and who have embraced the holy Mission of obeying, by vow, the precept of the Divine Zeal of the Heart of JESUS, *Rogate ergo Dominum.*[138]

Oh! what joy for you! my daughters in Jesus Christ. MÉLANIE, the Very Holy MARY's daughter of predilection, the sage, noble, and amiable creature has been the Educator and in some way the founder of your humble Institute.

You can never forget what a happy day it was when she first came among us. It was September 14, 1897, the fifth day of the novena of Our Lady of La Salette, the Holy day of Exaltation of the Holy Cross; admirable but inevitable coincidence on the part of Her who, on the mountain of La Salette, had seen the Very Holy Virgin and had to change her name to that of Sister Mary of the Cross. It was 10 o'clock in the morning when Sister Mary of the Cross presented herself at this place of the Holy Spirit, I was waiting for her on the sill of this Holy Temple. On seeing her, I could not help exclaiming to myself: whence comes such honor that a preferred daughter of the Mother of GOD should come and find me? But she, getting down on her knees, asked for the benediction of the priest, then she entered into the house of the Lord and participated in a profound communion of the Very Holy

---

[138] *Rogate ergo Dominum*: Matthew 9:38.

Sacrifice of Mass. All of you, my sisters, as well as
you orphans, you were waiting for her in the large
meeting hall. You were in holy anticipation, as if,
through an earthly creature, you were about to see the
Very Holy Virgin in person. And not only see her, but
have her in your midst; what a maternal guide and
what a Mistress! On her entry, accompanied by me,
you fell to your knees, seized with respect and affection, and you asked her for her blessing.

But the humble servant of the Lord, confused,
prostrated herself on the ground and asked for a
blessing from the minster of GOD for her and for you.
Such was her arrival at our poor Institute.

I do not wish to recount for you any more of
the marvels she operated here. My GOD! we have
been witnesses to all manner of uncommon acts! Everything in that creature was new and often mystical.
Assuredly the virtue that was within her and transpierced her recalled the lives of the Saints. From the
start, she was of such a charming innocence: she was
a very pure dove that seemed to have hovered above
all human miseries without having been touched by a
single drop of them. She was a scented lily of virgini-
ty, she was a very small child leaving the baptismal
font, but rich in prudence and wisdom. More than
once, we saw the birds enter into the Monastery and
come as far as her room, as if they were looking to
frolic with her.

The spirit of mortification and penance that
animated her was remarkable. She took excessively
little nourishment, scarcely several ounces, and absorbed it in small bites. At Galatina, a kilogram of

bread lasted her two weeks. Among us, she scarcely ate one or two ounces a day. She drank similarly very little, and never in large gulps. Before being among us, she had gone for three days a week consecutively without drinking, and said: "There is such great thirst in the world!" On Easter Sunday we have seen her solemnize that great Feast at the table, by taking half an egg! Never a piece of fruit, never a sweet. Her sleep never went beyond three hours and always on the bare ground, as you were able to confirm, my sisters. How many times, in the calm of the night, have you seen her pass, a light in hand, through the hallways! What shall we say of the macerations on her virginal flesh? What did those linen mean, which were covered with fresh blood at the shoulders, and which you had occasion to discover while taking her clothes to have them washed? What did that table of protruding nails, in the shape of a cross, signify, which gave one a shiver and which we keep with the small traces of blood on them?

Nonetheless, calm, serene, tranquil, consumed by virtue and suffering, on the outside she seemed unphased by anything; gracious and delicate in her bearing, her manners and the language she used, and as if the contrasts had been harmonized in her, she was welcoming and sociable, humble and imposing, amiable and reserved, strong and submissive, and she who had remained a very little child seemed superior to any mature and adult person. She was, in reality, simple like the dove and prudent like the serpent.[139]

I wish I had the language of an angel to speak

---

[139]*simple... serpent*: see Matthew 10:16.

to you about our MÉLANIE and to give you an idea of her ardent love for Our Lord JESUS CHRIST and the Very Holy Virgin MARY. In truth, her life was a life of love! She loved GOD with a pure love, and the flames of that mystical fire consumed her sometimes more, other times less. All the senses, all the fibers, all the faculties of that creature of GOD shivered with love. You remember with what transport of love she was nourished, for an entire day, on JESUS of the Holy Sacrament. This was her expression: "What I love, I would like to eat!"

Ah! I put her love for the Holy Sacrament to the test one day when, unexpectedly and without her expecting it, I prevented her from approaching the Holy Communion. She shuddered, felt ill, and fell to the ground as if dead. It was then that I could have an idea of what it was to be a veritable spirit of virtue, when, having regained her senses, she appeared for all the rest of the day so sweet, so humble, so mellow, and even more; and nevertheless, you could not help having a habitual admiration for her. But the pure love of GOD engenders zeal for his glory and for the salvation of souls. Zeal, said the Saint Bishop of Geneva,[140] is the fire of charity.[141] Great was the zeal that burned in the virginal heart of Mélanie. She would have wished to immolate herself with each passing moment so that GOD might be glorified, JESUS known and loved everywhere, and all souls sanctified

---

[140]Saint Bishop of Geneva: possibly a reference to the 5th century Salonius, who was canonized a Saint.

[141]charity: in the Christian sense, scil., *caritas* (love, affection, great kindness).

and saved. Her vivid faith and her ardent zeal made her consider priests like *new Christs*, and made her desire that the World be filled with true Ministers of the Sanctuary.

I have no doubt that, for that reason, she keenly loved our humble Institute, and that, from the moment she got familiar with it, she carried it in her heart forever, making it the object of her ardent prayers, because we had taken for our motto and our mission that great phrase of the Gospel, that celestial precept issued from the divine zeal of the Heart of Jesus: *Rogate ergo Dominum Messis ut mittat operarios in Messem suam.*

Oh! my Sisters, that prayer that you devoutly recite every day, how close she kept it to her heart! she saw in this humble institution that left her hands and in that spirit of prayer something like the precursor of her dear foundation of the new Apostles or Missionaries of the Mother of God. She wanted even to attach to her clothing the scapular of the Heart of Jesus bearing this sacred phrase, which formed our motto: "Pray ye therefore the Lord of the harvest, that he will send forth laborers into his harvest,"[142] and it will not be you, or me, my sisters, who give the lie to that comment that she made to me one day, in French: "*Je suis de votre Congrégration.*"[143]

I renounce trying to describe the marvels that you or I have been witness to while Mélanie stayed

---

[142]Matthew 9:38.

[143]*Je... Congrégration*: French for "I am a member of your Congregation."

with us. I say nothing of her sudden contemplations, in which she seemed to be out of her senses, as if ravished in ecstasy; nothing of that sort of divination of hearts that allowed her to read hidden thoughts, nothing of the two or three healings of orphans that resulted from her making a sign of the Cross, nothing of her extraordinary confidence in the Very Holy Virgin, by grace of whom she seemed always to have in her possession, and at the desired time, objects, nourishment or money, according to the needs of the House. Let us keep our silence on all that, and let us not prejudice in any way the authorized judgments that belong to the authority of the Church to make.

... It passed so quickly for us, the time that MÉLANIE of La Salette spent with us! The day of her departure came: she was deeply saddened. You remember with what humility she prostrated herself, asking your pardon with great cries; and you, with bitter lament, but alas! more comprehensible than hers, you did as she did! "Mother," you said to her, "between your sobs, will you remember us? will you put in a good word for us to the Lord?" And she: "yes, my children, I will always keep you in my heart; I will always pray for you... I leave for you as your superior, the Very Holy Virgin."

From Messina she went to Moncalieri; from Moncalieri, to France. She was in Diou; she was in Cusset. But one day she said, "I do not wish to remain in France; *I do not want to die among the Free Masons*." It was then that she resolved to return to her dear Italy, to find some isolated refuge where nobody knew her, where in silence and in solitude she could prepare for death. From that moment, the fires of divine love had become irresistible in her; she felt herself strongly attracted by Heaven.

Altamura, in the province of Bari, happy and blessed city, was the terminus of her earthly pilgrimages. She arrived there in June 1904. She was 72 years old then, and she was as if at the end of her strength. His Eminence Mgr. Cecchini, the very worthy Bishop of the two dioceses of Altamura and Acquaviva, gave her a great welcome: he knew what a treasure God was sending to his episcopal town! On the insistent prayers of the Servant of the Lord, he faithfully kept the secret of her arrival. He entrusted her, without naming her, to the noble and pious family of Gianuzzi who in no time confirmed the extraordinary sanctity of that admirable foreigner, and rather quickly began to love her as well as to venerate her; but She who, detached from all earthy affection, and chased away from her maternal home even, had kept the first years of her early childhood to herself, in silence and in secrecy, God destined her to die in a narrow room, in total abandonment, far from the presence, far from the assistance of any human creature.

It is his custom, God's, to reveal to his dear servants the day and the hour of their death. Had he reserved that grace for the Very Holy Virgin's favorite? We do not know. It is important to know, however, that MÉLANIE CALVAT, three months before her death, quit the pious Gianuzzi family while humbly expressing her thanks for their cordial hospitality, and retired to a small quarter of the city, the most out-of-the-way place, where she was more easily able to hide from all regards. Every morning she went to the Cathedral to hear the Holy Mass given, and nourished herself on "her dear friend the Eucharist." On the mere sight of her, the faithful were in admiration before that stranger's deep contemplation.

On December 15 of that same year, 1904, day eight of the worldwide feast of the Immaculate Conception, and on the eve of the preliminary novena of Noel, the Servant of the Lord was not seen at Church.

Mgr. the Bishop hastened to dispatch a valet to her home to look in on her, to see if she had need of anything. He knocked on the door: no response. He knocked again, knocked loudly this time: again, no response. He went quickly to inform Monseigneur who, suspecting some grave accident, alerted the civil authorities. The latter showed up at her door, confirmed that nobody responded, broke open the door, and entered.

The Servant of the Lord was lying lifeless on the bare floor.

They die in that way, great saints whom the Church has honored with altars; Saint Paul the hermit and Saint Mary the Egyptian, in the desert; Saint Francis Xavier, on a beach; and in a stable, Saint Germaine Cousin, that shepherd of France whose life has many resemblances to MÉLANIE'S life.

Let us note however that God's mercy, that Providence, full of love for those who love him, had already made preparations for his servant. In France, before her departure for Altamura, she had been on the verge of dying, and, as if on her death bed, she had received the holy Viaticum and Extreme Unction. Oh! blessed are those whose life is with Jesus, whose life is spent in the love of Jesus! *Beati mortui qui in Domino moriuntur...*[144] She had lived poor, solitary, penitent; she had desired only to be forgotten: alone with God! She wanted to die as she had been born!

But will we learn of the discoveries, delicate and full of love, made by her Beloved, by him who is faithful and true, in those solemn moments? Who will tell us of the succor, full of affection, given by the Immaculate One, by her who, on the mountain of La Salette, had shown herself, so beautiful and so majestic! And that recomforting assistance brought by the angels, her brothers? All that has been hidden from men's eyes...

Mélanie's death was like the condensed image of her life![145]

---

[144]*Beati... moriuntur.* Latin for "Blessed are those who die in the Lord."

[145]Original footnote: Mélanie was often given communion by Our Lord himself and enjoyed the constant view of her guardian angel. Now, two residents of Altamura have affirmed to having heard come from the apartment of the "pious French lady" at the time of the evening Angelus, on the night she died, angelic songs to the tune of *Pange lingua*, and the ringing of a bell as when one brings the Holy Viaticum.

Before an audience who knew that testimony, the orator kept within the bounds of insinuation only, and the solemnity of the funeral oration demanded discretion. Someone wrote to him to confirm the deposition of those two witnesses, or to officially deny it.

Here is his response:

But it would be a mistake to read into that death on the bare floor the simple, unexpected consequence of a syncope. No! Her bed, – she never slept in it, that servant of God, innocent and penitent. We have already mentioned how it was on the bare floor that she took her repose and her sleep, for several hours during the night,... Is it not the case to exclaim: *Moriatur anima mea morte justorum?*[146] That "of the righteous," – could we die as she died? Would that the end of our life might be like hers!

Adieu, so beautiful soul! *Adieu*, creature of love, complete work of love, of the very pure and very holy love of Jesus, the Sovereign Good! *Adieu*, vigilant and prudent Virgin! When, in the calm of the night, the voice of the Spouse called out to you, without delay, you ran to It, with the mystical Lamp, the lamp filled with oil and shining splendorously!... For you, the tasks are completed, the long and fatiguing trips, the exhausting pilgrimages, the profound agonies of love, of holy Love, with its insatiable hunger and its inextinguishable thirst for the Justice that does

---

"I certify to you that it is really true that the gentleman Pascal Massari, of Altamura, respectable individual, worthy in the faith, and a woman, Mélanie's neighbors, have affirmed to me (and are ready to take an oath) having heard, the first, the song *Pange lingua* that accompanied angelic voices, with the ringing of a bell; the other a continuous sound of a bell as when someone carries the Holy Viaticum.

"I have received these depositions in the presence of two priests among my friends, of which one is a Frenchman, after having asked of those individuals minute and precise questions."

[146]*Moriatur... justorum*: Latin for "Let me die the death of the righteous." Numbers 23:10.

not inhabit this earth! At this hour, it is the Almighty that is your inheritance!... Yes, that thought is very sweet to us: the expiatory flames were not for you, or at least your passage there was fleet, and now there you are for eternity, entered into the joy of your God! Yes, they are realized in happiness, those ardent desires for endless union with the Lord who so often wrested this cry from you: "When will the hour come? Oh! the hour, when will it come?..." Rest in joy, dilate your heart in the beatific vision of that Jesus, the object of your sighs, the perpetual aspiration of your soul filled with love, that Jesus whom you never had any fear of following in his sorrowful tracks! His cross, it was delights, smiles, and joy for you, the "flower that never withers," you often wrote! Oh! like the Spouse in the Song of Songs, how many times have you languished with love for your Beloved! It was a fire that leapt out of your breast!...And when, having entered into the kingdom of Eternal Glory, when you saw the immaculate Queen, She who had as if driven your child's heart crazy with love, so tender and so full of trust, when you let out this cry: "*Madonna mia! Madonna mia!*" by which you acclaimed the Great Queen... all that, how could I describe it!...

O MÉLANIE, from that elevated throne that God has seated you on in Heaven, does your glance still fall to earth? Will you always love us with that heart that so loved us in these lowly places of exile? But what I am saying? Does not all love in the here-below grow perfected in its contact with God? Is it possible that in Heaven the Blessed do not love those who love them? Yes! In God you love us... One day, when you were among these poor orphans, someone said to you, "Mother (they gave you that name), Mother, once you leave, you will no longer think of us." "Ah!" you replied, "you do not know my heart!"

At this hour in time, in the Kingdom of Eternal Love, when you love us with perfect Charity, ah! do not stop praying for us. Pray for all those who venerate you like a celestial being. Pray for these virgins, "the Daughters of the Divine Zeal," for whose religious education you spent one year of your life, with more than maternal care, with a wise and enlightened direction, with a most particular zeal to set them on the way of the Lord. You know it, you know that these pious girls consecrated to the Very Holy Heart of Jesus and devoted by you yourself to Mary, the Immaculate Mother, – you know that they regarded you like a delegate of the Very Holy Virgin come into their midst, seven years ago, and who seemed never to have left them.

And on me also, on me who bring this feeble tribute of homage in memory of you, on me who received so many demonstrations of your very noble heart, your pure and saintly dilection, on me also deign to lavish the powerful assistance of your prayers to the adorable Redeemer Jesus Christ and to Mary his Immaculate Mother!...

Other Books by the Publisher

Fanchette's Pretty Little Foot by Restif de La Bretonne

Je M'Accuse... by Léon Bloy

My Hospitals & My Prisons by Paul Verlaine

Salvation Through the Jews by Léon Bloy

Words of a Demolitions Contractor by Léon Bloy

Cellulely by Paul Verlaine

Flowers of Bitumen by Émile Goudeau

Songs for Her & Odes in Her Honor by Paul Verlaine

On Huysmans' Tomb by Léon Bloy

Ten Years a Bohemian by Émile Goudeau

The Soul of Napoleon by Léon Bloy

Blood of the Poor by Léon Bloy

Theresa the Philosopher & The Carmelite Extern Nun by Marquis d'Argens & Anne-Gabriel Meusnier de Querlon

A Platonic Love by Paul Alexis

Two Novellas: Francine Cloarec's Funeral and Benjamin Rozes by Léon Hennique

The Revealer of the Globe: Christopher Columbus & His Future Beatification (Part One) by Léon Bloy

Joan of Arc and Germany by Léon Bloy

Héloïse Pajadou's Calvary by Lucien Descaves

An Immodest Proposal by Dr. Helmut Schleppend

The Pornographer by Restif de La Bretonne

Style (Theory and History) by Ernest Hello

On the Threshold of the Apocalypse: 1913-1915 by Léon Bloy